D1483295

Determined To Live

BRIAN HESSION

Determined
To Live

DOUBLEDAY & COMPANY, INC.

GARDEN CITY, NEW YORK

1957

B

Hession

Library of Congress Catalog Card Number 57–7284

Copyright 1956 by Brian Hession
All Rights Reserved
Printed in the United States of America
First Edition

Dedicated to
DR. JOHN HOWARD PAYNE
of Pasadena, California,
who was not only my surgeon
and doctor but also my friend.

With grateful thanks to the Good Samaritan Hospital of the Episcopal Church, Los Angeles, and to Mary Pickford and the Bishop and the many church congregations of Los Angeles and other dioceses who subscribed to pay my hospital expenses in August 1954.

O God, MAY the message of this book be
WIDE ENOUGH to include
All who need divine love
And human fellowship,
NARROW ENOUGH to shut out
All envy, pride and strife.
MAY its words be
KIND ENOUGH to be
No stumbling block
To sufferers or
To straying feet, YET
RUGGED AND STRONG enough
To turn back
The tempter's power.
O God, MAY the readers of this book find
Courage and faith so to live in this world,
That they reach the very gateway
To Thine everlasting Kingdom,
Through Jesus Christ our Lord. Amen.

Foreword

By The Right Reverend Cuthbert K. N. Bardsley,
Lord Bishop of Coventry

WEARERS of the Victoria Cross have come from all parts of the world for the Centenary celebrations—their bravery has elicited the admiration of millions.

But courage is not confined to the battlefields of war. Every hospital is a battlefield and courage is to be found in every ward. The highest degree of courage is that which is demonstrated over a long period of time, that goes on going on.

This is a courageous book: its author has been through the valley of the shadow of death and through the equally dreaded marshes of a slow and painful convalescence. Out of his sufferings he has written a book that will challenge, stimulate and comfort thousands. Here are no pious platitudes. Here is no escapist message. This is a book written out of the personal experience of shock, pain, disappointment, fear, and constant weakness. But it is a story of victory—the victory of faith, the victory of determination. The author is a man whose faith in Jesus Christ has been deepened and enriched by suffering. His faith was tried and tested, but not found wanting. He commends this faith to you.

This is a book you may not want to read. But once you have begun, you will not want to put it down. It may challenge, convict, and annoy you, but in the end it will, I hope, bring home to you the words of St. Peter; "that the trial of your faith, being much more precious than of gold that perisheth, though it be tried with fire, might be found unto praise and honour and glory at the appearing of Jesus Christ."

CUTHBERT COVENTRY

30th June, 1956.

CONTENTS

Introduction to the American Edition

THIS book was published in Britain on September 3, 1956, and the first edition of ten thousand copies was sold out in the first ten days. Publication followed in five other countries and to my surprise the medical profession, instead of resenting a layman's intrusion on the subject of cancer, welcomed it and obtained copies to give to their patients and their relatives. Clergy and other sympathizers with the Cancer Anonymous concept pooled lists of indigent suffering patients, fearful individuals, and strategically placed persons, so that they were given a copy.

A nationwide advertising-company director after reading the book donated the total services of his vast organisation to design and print enormous forty-eight-sheet posters in colour, and from October onwards exhibited them free of charge on his billboards throughout London and Britain.

Such immediate reactions were more than I had dared to dream, and a new world of pastoral service has opened to me. I have knelt and prayed with many whose problems are far greater than my own and it is encouraging to know that this book is being of service to others. It is always very humbling to be instrumental in helping—in person, in sermons, or in print—a fellow human being during the hour of his trouble. I am grateful for the spontaneous help of so many people in different walks of life.

I have lived for the day when this book would be pub-

lished in my beloved America, despite its English flavour.
I am sure there will be many who will rise up to help forward its message and already I have opened an account
in Los Angeles for the giving of copies to indigent patients.
Thus I shall have many an American partner helping to
bring renewed hope, courage, and faith amid this field of
human suffering which touches every family. No one
would suggest that America lacks any medical services for
the relief of cancer, and I know that vast reserves of funds
have been generously donated for cancer research, but one
thing above all others we need to be constantly reminded
of, and that is the paramount importance of the spiritual
hope and determination of the individual person. People
matter . . . they matter to God and to each one of us if
we are among those who care for the individual rather
than the machine.

The National Society for Cancer Relief in Britain—one
of our oldest societies—very generously paid for twin air-
plane tickets from coast to coast of America for my wife
and me, and in October 1956 sent me on a cancer fact-
finding tour.

For eight weeks we flew from city to city, from New
York and Toronto right across to Colorado Springs, San
Francisco, and Los Angeles. We had the most wonderful
welcome everywhere, expecially among the leading cancer
specialists, who were only too anxious to sit down and discuss the problems, our hopes for the future, and the need
for stimulating the faith of the individual in the battle
against cancer. We have all so much to learn from one
another . . . so much to do in life that is worth while. I
listened and learned at hospitals, cancer research places,
and local cancer societies. I spoke at medical meetings,
preached in churches and on the radio. I was impressed
by all I saw of the cancer work and took back an interesting report to share with our leading men. We piled up

more memories of American scenery and an increasing circle of friends.

I was particularly thrilled to see my surgeon again in Los Angeles and with him I inspected hospitals, attended cancer autopsies, and watched a few operations. I look forward to returning to America many times to speak and to preach. With the backing of the press, doctors, and ministers, I would like to conduct big thanksgiving services in church in certain big cities. There are thousands of cured cancer patients who are living happy useful lives for which they are deeply grateful.

I arrived back in England to be greeted by a tornado of work, for the Cancer Anonymous postbag had grown out of all proportion and this was even further increased when the B.B.C. presented my life on TV in "This Is Your Life." For this they flew Dr. Payne and my nurse over the North Pole from Hollywood to the utter astonishment of the twenty million British who were looking in. The programme, while it was embarrassing for me, helped many to realise almost for the first time in Britain that CANCER CAN BE CURED OR ENDURED.

The final aim and dream I have for Britain is to help Cancer Anonymous to inspire the creation of a united BRITISH CANCER SOCIETY out of the present chaos. Almost overnight has come the ever growing support of the top cancer men and members of Parliament. What I learned in your country of the wonderful American Cancer Society is standing me in good stead. Plans are afoot at this moment for me to have a TV series: "From Parson to Patient." So I would ask your prayers for me as we bring about a new day for present cancer patients in Britain, and maybe in other countries. I have been invited to visit South Africa and Australia, but it is America which is like a big magnet drawing me. In fact I have signed a Colston Leigh lecture contract for ten weeks each fall for the next three years. This will envolve four engagements a week in different American cities.

I hope that the great American reading public will accept this simple book by one who loves their country and is extremely grateful to God for a new lease of life, and that through them this book will inject into the vast cancer field a new spiritual directive. I pray it will reach those who may find within its pages something to invigorate them, whether they be hale and hearty or sick and dying. The message of this book is for everyone and not just for the cancer patient. Two further books are nearly completed during the night watches: *Alone to Pray*, a bedside book of prayers and thoughts, and *Man Must Fight*.

We all need a faith to live without self-pity, and we all need a faith to die with grace and dignity.

February 1957

The Rev. Brian Hession, M.A.

Cancer Anonymous
Dawn Trust
c/o All Saints Church
Beverly Hills, California

From a Hospital Bed

I AM writing this from my bed in the Good Samaritan Hospital in Los Angeles by means of a tape recorder which is sitting on a table alongside my bed. It is not easy at this moment to dictate this rather personal story, for only a few days ago I had an extensive operation for internal cancer, and I still have the tube through my nose and on down into my stomach, tubes feeding drips of saline and other ingredients into my veins, first into one arm and then into another—in fact, I have tubes in all directions. The tube down my nose is rather uncomfortable, but it is a great help, for it prevents my being sick, and by means of a Rube Goldberg contraption it removes all the usual flatulence.

I want to convey these thoughts to you on the subject of cancer and faith in Christ now at this particular moment, so that they may be a comfort to others in trouble and in like pain. These thoughts and arguments are really addressed not only to fellow cancer sufferers and relatives but to all who have to endure pain of body and mind or bereavement and the resultant battle to continue to believe in a God of *Love* as Christ revealed Him.

I do not want you to feel that these words were said or written by someone in the pink of health or who had already recovered from a great illness and was looking back on it—forgetting the bad parts and remembering only the good.

There are moments in the lives of most of us when we need to take time off to consider our faith, and it is not always easy for a priest to say the kind of things which can strengthen trust in God when he knows that his hearer may be going through great agony, while he, at the bedside, is fit and well.

Some of us cry out against God the moment we are in pain, as if God were to blame or at least at fault for allowing it. Of course, it is far easier to rebel against God in the face of the challenge of pain and say, "Why does God *allow* the excruciating agony of cancer?"

That is a question I have often been asked, and I have noted the tone of defiance and antagonism in the patients' voices. It is as if they are saying under their breath: "You sit there in your dog collar and talk glibly about God, but you don't know what pain is like. Would you still believe if this monstrous thing happened to you?" Suffering does make some people very rebellious against God and the "revolt of Youth" against God, parents and any kind of authority is lighthearted by comparison.

It is all too easy to become sour and bitter in all life's relationships. That is a great waste of happiness, draining reserves which should be conserved to fight pain and help the doctors.

If I wait till I am well before I write this I may not be able to remember just what it feels like to be in the middle of a crisis, hanging on to God by one's teeth. Besides, my brain is bursting with thoughts to share with others.

It may be wondered how it is that I have a tape recorder at my bedside. It is here for a very personal reason. It was lent to me by a friend a week ago, when I had just been told that I had the last and extreme stages of cancer of the rectum and intestines. In case I had to meet my

Maker, I wanted to have a few moments the night before
my double operation in which I could record a message in
my own living voice to my wife, my two young children,
my mother-in-law, and my mother. There was so much to
say and so little time in which to say it all, and I was too
tired to write. I hoped that if I had died they would be
able to hear my voice talking to them as it had talked in
life. But I didn't die and this modern toy at my side has a
far better use. With it I hope that my thoughts and feelings at this time, when they are strangely lucid, and while
I am still traversing the jungle of suffering with its strain
on a continuing trust in Christ, will be of help to others.
Maybe it is that I am wondering if I shall ever be able to
preach again, and so the idea of this book becomes very
important to me. I hope it will reach where I can never go
and there bring renewed hope, faith, and courage.

As a parson I have stood by the bedside of so many and
ached to be able to share with them my own trust in Christ,
but I have had the words dry on my lips, for I wondered
sometimes whether I had the right to tell others of a spiritual ointment for suffering when I had not *yet* proved it
strong enough to endure my own baptism of deep suffering. Now I am so grateful to God to be alive that I am
determined to live in order to help others.

During the Sunday before the operation, my wife and I
let this tape recorder run while we had our last hours together and talked about all those lovely nostalgic memories which two people in love always possess: of holidays,
of many friends, of that utter feeling of oneness and con-
tentment in the physical worship of one another. We remembered together the financial struggles and the thrill of
watching a life's work on religious visual aids grow to
maturity and nationwide acceptance. Vivid pictures came
to our minds of places and people we had loved . . . of our
romantic Goathorn cottage by the sea in Poole Harbour,

and the happy lazy sailing days in our small sailing boat in the English Channel.

What precious hours these were before the storm, when we lived our lives over and over again and enjoyed every minute of them. God had been good to us and we prayed and gave thanks to Him and asked for a continuation of life.

Apart from her own memories, my wife now has that tape recording of our talks together, and I assured her then—as I assured my children in the next recording—that I was not in the very least afraid to die and to meet God. Not because I thought I had done anything particularly good: indeed, there is so very much all of us regret having done, so many things that we all feel we could have done for God and our fellow men.

But, over and above everything else, there is the tremendous conviction that the Christ of God died for us and promised us forgiveness. This was and is my sure hope, for otherwise the whole of life is meaningless.

One salient point of all stands out in bold relief to me: namely, that the Christian, when he passes from this world, has nothing to fear.

He is to be greeted by one who loves him, knows the worst about him, has forgiven him and has died for him. Take this away, and I am lost and afraid; and death itself, instead of being a release and freedom, has a sting in it as ruthless as the world of evil men and women.

No doubt when we meet Him He will have plenty to say to us about the things we have done or left undone, but there will be His hand in ours, and in His strength and sovereignty He will take us to the throne of God.

Strange how it all seems so very near and familiar when the body draws towards the parting of the ways. I found myself looking forward to knowing the mystery which surrounds the Creator of the Universe, looking forward to

meeting fellow Christians and those whom I had been permitted to lead closer to God during my twenty-seven
years in His service.

Stronger than any desire to be parted from a tired body
is the tremendous urge to live—to have more time in which
to create something worth while. It bubbles up from
within, and it helps the pains to be talking into this little
microphone. It suddenly becomes all-important to me to
create a book which may help others in need, and I pray I
may live long enough to finish it and to see it published.

CHAPTER 1

A Visit to America

MY mother was a Protestant—Church of England—so my brother and I were duly baptised into the Church of England.

My father died when I was about eight, so my mother had a tough job on her hands to bring up two boys at boarding school, and little did she know that both were going to turn out to be preachers of the Gospel.

Like most small boys I was pretty "anti-God," and not being at a day school, I did not have to go to Sunday school; but at the age of fourteen I met Bishop Taylor Smith, who became almost a second father to me. Once a man like Taylor Smith gets his hands on you, you do not escape; and so it was that at this tender age I was converted—much to the amusement of my brother. When I was sixteen I decided that God wanted me to be a parson, and a howl of disapproval went up from my family, who could ill afford a university training and had an office job in mind for me. "A widow's son going to be a parson is ridiculous. There's no money in it," was their verdict, so I had to set about getting a scholarship to Cambridge, and eventually I won them over. Just about this time my brother Roy was converted and grew up to be a robust and graphic free-lance preacher, eventually throwing in his lot with the Reverend Billy Graham.

As I look back on life, I do not think I enjoyed my public-school days very much, but my student period stands out as the most enjoyable time of all, and friends made during this time still occupy a very warm place in my affections. Only a few months ago I conducted an undergraduate mission in Holy Trinity Church, Cambridge, and experienced the thrill of visiting my old rooms in the Fellows' Building at Christ's College—rooms which held so many memories and were once occupied by Milton when he wrote *Paradise Lost*.

Cambridge, with its superb buildings, lives on in quiet majesty and dignity, shaping the lives of young people for a world that is topsy-turvy. Why Americans, touring Britain, so often visit Oxford and miss the beauty of Cambridge, I never understand. What could be finer than a city consisting almost entirely of college after college right next door to one another, with a curling river running through the lawns of the colleges?

As I lie in bed I can transport myself back to Cambridge with ease, into King's College Chapel with its twinkling candle lights and the red-robed choir singing Evensong; or in imagination walk again along the Backs by the side of the river, to gaze at the succession of beautiful buildings.

My student days were interspersed with helping in missions and running camps for schoolboys from the slums or from public schools.

We used to take a hundred boys to winter sports in Switzerland for only fourteen pounds for fourteen days, including the fare. At Easter we would hire yachts on the Norfolk Broads and teach the boys to sail. The whole idea behind these efforts was to "convert" the boys to a sane, healthy, personal faith in a living Christ. There would be voluntary prayers in the evenings. One of us would talk and try to present the Christian message in a more informal way than they heard it in school chapels. Boys hero-worship, so we chose our undergraduate staff carefully so that it included a fair proportion of Blues—athletes who represented their university at some sport. The idea was to show that being a Christian was not an occupation for dull dogs, but for those in full command of their faculties.

In my day at Cambridge, about half the Blues were identified Christians. When I got a Blue for swimming and water polo, I think I valued it more than my degree.

Even in those days, however, I was made aware of the scourge of cancer. Two of my best friends in our mission work, well-known running Blues, while still in training, died of cancer of the lung.

I myself had a motor accident and had to rest for a year in Italy and North Africa. Thanks to the late Dr. Garbett, who was to become Archbishop of York, I was ordained without the necessity of passing any ordination examinations and I became a curate to the late Canon F. H. Gillingham who was one of the most outstanding preachers in the Church in London. His church was always crowded, with two services every Sunday night and a congregation of more than a thousand at each. He was a master man who taught me to read the Bible in church as if it was a piece of live dramatic literature to command the attention of everyone. He also insisted that we, his curates, learnt all the services by heart—especially the wedding service, so that (as he put it), "You can give your undivided attention to the bride and bridegroom without a head buried in a book." To all of us he taught that the typical parson's voice was a sign of immaturity and lack of schooling for the job, or else downright affectation. All this was to stand me in good stead as a Royal Air Force chaplain, and when I was made vicar of Holy Trinity, Aylesbury, the county town of Buckinghamshire, where I stayed for thirteen years.

As a vicar one learns a great deal about human nature and suffering; and to be a vicar offers a great opportunity for doing something to win people to the Christian faith and to build them into the community of Christian life around a parish church.

A vicar or rector has to be a Jack-of-all-trades and is expected to be a good preacher, a good visitor, a good writer of parish magazines, good with children, and in fact good with everyone. He learns, too, the difficult task of collecting money from people who have lost the art of giving, in order to keep his church solvent. It is awful to think that all the "good works" of our world are restricted and slowed down through lack of money, and some people imagine that the Church of England is paid for by the State! This is not so, and in point of fact, past endowments by the wills of faithful people are yielding smaller and smaller returns, while the cost of living rises; and the present generation has to be taught that it must bear its share and not rely on the past.

I chose the Church of England because, looking on as a young man, I found within it a community of Christians with the least amount of human error. As I see things, all man-made institutions are imperfect, and none of us claims for any of our churches a state of perfection, nor the exclusive possession of the Gospel.

Only in Christ is there perfection, for we know that in Him is the image and likeness of God. Humankind is made up of such a tremendous variety of temperaments that it would be very unreasonable that all should be regimented to worship God in exactly the same form and mode.

Churches are reputed to be slow in adapting themselves to changing conditions and new methods. My life's work has been to create the visual approach in the spread of Christianity.

It has been said that 80 per cent of absorbed education

comes through the eye, which creates picture memories of knowledge and belief in the very citadel of the subconscious mind. When I was still at Cambridge I took an honours degree in history as well as a medical course in tropical disease and hygiene in case I should become a missionary. I attended medical lectures which ended with a motion-picture film summary of the lecture. This set me working at doing something similar for the Christian message. Starting at the very bottom with a silent 35-mm. camera and projector, I began to create the basis of what has now become the religious film movement.

For twenty-five years I have pioneered this field on a shoestring budget with no capital resources. It has not been easy. There has been plenty of criticism and it is far easier to criticise than to create. But the work has gone on, and more clergy and teachers have been converted to our new way of reaching people.

In 1933, while a curate, I began the foundation of the Dawn Trust as an organisation or fellowship, registered as a charity, to make, supply, and promote films and strips for use by Christian leaders of any denomination. It was hard slogging work up and down the country, fighting against prejudice and apathy: and during the war years we gave hundreds of religious film services in air-raid shelters. I think back on these years of effort, making films, humping projectors around to churches for film missions or clergy conferences in order to convert the godless and woo the clergy, and I know that it has all been worth while.

During the struggle to get the new method over to the public, I not only had to contend with lack of money but the overcoming of prejudice. I had to win over the intelligent but obstinate minds to my way of thinking, and then they became useful supporters in the years to come. It is never any good to wear a chip on your shoulder because at first people do not agree, but one must listen to their points of view and then win them over by sheer sincerity.

The Church of England is a very slow and difficult body to move. At a time when one of my films had been banned by the London County Council, Queen Mary sent for me from Marlborough House and she asked if she could see the film. In fact she went a stage further and attended the première which the then Bishop of London (Dr. Winnington Ingram) very kindly held in his palace in an effort to defeat the London County Council.

The Queen was very frank and over a cup of tea afterwards announced that she could see no objection to the film in any cinema provided it was not preceded by a Mickey Mouse. Turning to me with a twinkle in her eye, she said, "Young man, you can make my presence known to the press and public if that will help you at all."

To the chagrin of certain Church committees, the national newspapers the next day splashed the headline that Queen Mary had attended a sacred film première in the presence of Lord Camrose, the Bishop of London, and all sorts of important people.

The incident made a few enemies, and a few years later when I held what was said to be the first religious film service complete with film, hymns, and prayers, Queen Elizabeth, the present Queen's mother, sent a special message of good wishes for the endeavour and the whole movement. From then on opposition melted away, but the way has never been easy in this pioneer field.

The publicity in the national press in Britain and even in America has been extremely useful in educating the general public to accept religious films, but some newspaper stories have been very hard to take.

As a boy I spent many week-ends at Lord Beaverbrook's country home, Cherkley Court, so I learnt something, even in my young days, of the ballyhoo of newspapers, which stood me in good stead in the years that followed.

A newspaper reporter in New York in 1946 planted a completely ludicrous version of my visit to America next door to Eleanor Roosevelt's "My Day." The net result was that she asked me to lunch in her flat and we spent the rest of the day arguing about world problems and how to cope with them. True to her promise, she arranged all sorts of introductions with Nelson Rockefeller and many in the film city. While hopes often ran high for bigger plans, my feet had to be firmly planted on the ground while I was steadily building up an experienced body of film and film-strip users in Britain and the mission field.

There were many frustrations and anxious moments through lack of money. The poor struggling clergy and social workers in the slums could not be charged more for the use of the films and yet they looked to Dawn Trust to keep them supplied with the right material.

Today the Dawn Trust of Aylesbury supplies visual material to over ten thousand hard-working clergy and lay people who are members or users of the Trust. The tide has turned, and visual aids are the accepted way of teaching and preaching, and a projector for film or strips is as much part of the necessary equipment of a parish or Sunday school as an organ. Our material reaches the mission field, where one good biblical picture is worth a thousand words; and we have links with other people producing religious films in other countries. It is also used by all the free churches such as the Methodists and Baptists as well as the Roman Catholics; in fact we have a special department for the latter. Every State school now uses some of our films or strips. In point of fact, Dawn Trust was started twenty-three years ago by three of us—two Roman Catholics and myself.

The financial ramifications of the work are still pathetic, for such work can never be financially solvent when Dawn Trust has to produce religious films or purchase them from overseas, as well as distribute them at very low rentals to the churches. The work has obviously to be sponsored in the same way as an advertising or demonstration film, for it brings no box-office or financial return. To date there have been no sponsors, and donations have been very small, so the task has always been a problem of economics, and I have had to turn my hand to making all kinds of educational and travel films, chiefly in colour. These sell or hire all over the world, to produce a slow but steady income for our main objective.

The whole burden and responsibility of finding the money to keep things going has fallen on me, and such a burden is a very wearisome, lonely thing.

This religious film movement has the avowed object of harnessing the invention of motion pictures and a series of still pictures called film strips, to the service of Christian adventure—to the very church itself, for they are used in Sunday evening services, Sunday schools, and youth clubs.

The priority is to project the Gospel story and not to give pseudo-entertainment to the religious community. Life is too short to waste time on that sort of thing. The ordinary public cinema provides entertainment and make-believe, and the church cannot hope to compete with that.

It is wishful thinking to hope to get very much serious Christian ethics or direct evangelism through the public cinema type of films. Every now and again the moguls of the film industry give us a surfeit of so-called "religious" supers or big biblical epics, which tend to give a somewhat garbled version of a religious theme. Maybe they do some good, but they are not designed for use in the churches by the churches. The Roman Catholics in Hollywood have a most efficient office which gives advice and help to producers, in the hope of getting a greater degree of truth and accuracy. It is a pity that the Protestants do not do likewise.

As Chairman of the Dawn Trust of England, I was sent to America in May 1954 by a large combined group of clergy and ministers of all possible denominations. They subscribed to pay the fare, while I paid for the rest and for my wife. The main object, though I was also to preach, was that I should be spiritual technical adviser to a company which was making a wide-screen colour film built around the life of Jesus, *The Day of Triumph.* My job was to try to bring more spiritual integrity to the film, in the name of the British churches, and I worked during eight weeks of production without salary or expenses, so that I could be free to express the spiritual point of view. During the production I took four hundred colour transparencies with a view to making eight fine film strips and slides for use in Sunday schools. The quality of the American sunlight and studio lighting resulted in the most perfect pictures.

When I reached the Hal Roach studios in Hollywood, which had been hired, I found that it was a commercial company making the film, intent on making it a box-office success. Few people concerned had ever read their Bibles, so I had a tough job in trying to bring sincerity and spiritual integrity into the picture. I called for silence before some of the most sacred scenes and led actors and technicians in prayer. Everyone was terribly friendly, but the most ludicrous things happened both in the studios and out on location in the desert. The only other spiritual adviser—a Methodist minister from Texas, a member of whose church had put up a good deal of the money—turned up for one day in the middle of the shooting and promptly went home. I myself had the most terrible heart searchings over the film, although the wide-screen colour photography was superb, and some incidents called for great tact with the promoters. The director, Irving Pichel, died of a heart attack the day we saw the first rough cut, which was four hours long. I attended the first two cutting sessions before I came into this hospital and during these conferences I pleaded that they omit the extraneous matter which was not in the Bible and leave in the many really good parts. The final film is to be about two hours long.

What difference I managed to make, I do not know: some, I hope, for occasionally my advice was taken or I was assured that it would look all right on the screen.

My wife and I arrived by sea on May 1, 1954, and I preached without fees in many cities—New York, Chicago, Washington, Colorado Springs, Tyler in Texas, and then in California. I had been to America before, but never driven across it. We bought a new car, a Bel Air Chevrolet, at factory price and drove across America. We kept it for four months and, when we sold it to a garage in Los Angeles, it had not only cost us nothing, but we made £22. It was a dream car with no gears, foam seats, and the colour was turquoise and ivory. It was hard to say goodbye to it for it had been our moving home as we sped across America staying in motels and eating our lunch while one or other of us continued driving. If we had taken such a gorgeous car back to England it would have cost a fortune and there would have been many eyebrows raised if people saw a parson driving it. Our black Scottie would soon have covered the seats with good English mud, for he considers our car at home to be his moving kennel. We are fast drivers and are very used to long distances, having driven many times across Europe even amid snow to keep speaking engagements or to make documentary colour films. This experience stood us in good stead when tackling the vast distances in America.

We took our time crossing America, and everywhere we had the most fabulous welcome and saw the most wonderful scenery and met the most wonderful people. We fell even more in love with Americans than we had ever done before. The churches were packed, and everywhere we had a welcome fit for royalty. Americans have a wonderful sense of humour and gaiety.

It is very difficult to say which of the many places stand out most in our minds. It helps to enjoy them all over again as I lie here and call them to mind. We enjoyed New York, Washington, and Chicago, but the real thrills began when we spent a few days in the Rocky Mountain National Park in a small log cabin and drove up to the top of Pikes Peak—fourteen thousand feet. I admit we did not quite complete the last hundred yards, because it was snowing quite hard and the mists had come down, which made it difficult to see the edge of the narrow road, on one side of which there was a sheer drop. Our hearts were in our mouths a good deal of the way, and I did not want to take any more risks with a gearless new car above the snow line in the late afternoon. It was an amazing experience to drive a car in the air-line pilot's domain, at an altitude of twelve thousand feet. We threaded our way, almost aimlessly, on small roads through these lovely Rocky Mountains, passing deserted gold mines and gold-rush towns, down to Denver. Here we saw the fabulous natural open-air theatre of red sandstone where they hold an Easter Sunrise Service on Easter morning, amid the vast rocks that tower above the plains of Colorado.

It was almost a freewheel drive from there down to the sparkling city of Colorado Springs in which there is that gaiety in the air which belongs to sophisticated cities that enjoy a warm climate. The streets are delightfully laid out and packed with well-dressed people in gay summer frocks or highly coloured trousers.

I preached at Gracechurch for an old friend, the Reverend Lindsay Patton, and found the most warmhearted congregation that any man could wish for, and, what means more to a preacher, I was invited into their homes to have meals with them. I was even allowed into the kitchen after Sunday lunch to help wash up and this makes you feel part of the family. The servant problem is acute all over the world.

Going to church on a Sunday in America is not only the done thing, but it is a most enjoyable occasion—and so it should be. The minister or rector is around outside the church, before and after the service, to shake hands with everyone and to wish them well. Everyone knows everyone, and they are full of smiles and uninhibited good cheer. All are welcome to stay to the "Coffee Hour" after the service in the church patio. The ladies of the parish take it in turns to be hostesses to serve the coffee or ice cream. The preacher is introduced to everyone, and his diary of dates for breakfast, lunch, tea, and dinner is quickly filled up. How different it is in Britain!

The Americans, although they cannot always understand the sound tracks of British movies, like listening to a British voice in church, at Rotary lunches or at Yacht Club lunches. I enjoyed the unscripted radio broadcast talks and interviews. Americans respond quickly to a little bit of veiled wit and humour even in church, and I was surprised to find congregations suddenly rocking with laughter.

One day we took the evening off from social rounds and drove into the mountains. Stopping at a small place calling itself Bruin Inn, we were invited by the owner to dinner, and enjoyed a family party, complete with a pet porcupine which kept climbing up the chairs. Someone had just shot their pet bear, much to the children's distress. This was a homely evening, when we exchanged life histories to the accompaniment of huge beefsteaks. Yet we and our hosts had begun it as complete strangers.

In contrast, the rector and his wife took us on Saturday night to a dinner party at the magnificent Broadmoor Hotel at the foot of the Rockies on the edge of a lake, with beautiful marble terraces and a floodlit swimming pool where a bathing beauty competition was going on. Some beauties too!

The rector knew everyone and, what is more, everyone knew him and greeted him like an old family friend. The Americans respect "the cloth" and treat their clergy generously—half price on the railroads, cars at factory price, and 25-per-cent discount in the better-class shops.

The clergy are on the whole good types: they have to be to hold their jobs down. That evening ended with a private preview of a new colour film for half a dozen of us at midnight. Despite the gaiety, I was almost speechless at times with pain without anyone knowing it, and I was up all night in our room. I had come there to preach and spread happiness, and the enthusiastic congregation on the next day had not the slightest idea that their preacher was in the midst of "an attack."

After four days we drove on through the Royal Gorge, to Mesa Verde Mountain to inspect the Indian caves which are thousands of years old and are in a wonderful state of preservation.

From there we drove on Utah Desert tracks to an Indian Post in Monument Valley, which was a wonderful experience, for we arrived at night in the dark during a lightning storm without rain. The keeper of the Post wanted fourteen dollars a night for a bed, so we said we would sleep in the car—at which he softened up and let us have a couple of beds in a cattle shed complete with the marmots running everywhere. He seemed to like us because we were prepared to rough it rather than pay high prices.

"Do you want to get up at 4 A.M. in the morning and see the Indian sunrise ceremony?" he barked, but there was an increasing friendliness in his voice.

"We certainly would; and can we bring our movie and still cameras along?" I replied, feeling it was almost too good to be true, and although worn out from long driving in the dark we simply could not miss such an opportunity. First he checked with O'Connor, one of Walt Disney's cameramen, who was sitting in the dark on an old wooden balcony watching the lightning storm. We exchanged names and film-technician union cards, for we film people are cagey about treading on other people's preserves. Luckily I was an old friend of Disney's, so all was well, and before dawn the next morning we set forth in the old man's jeep with an Indian squaw sitting in the back. Across miles of utter wasteland and dried-up river beds we bumped our way, and what we saw has made a wonderful film of unrepeatable scenes.

Indians, except those who have sold themselves for show business in the towns in the hope of being able to buy drink from the liquor lockers, never allow themselves to be filmed. Our new-found friend had got over this difficulty, but it was touch-and-go once or twice, so I sat cross-legged on the red sand and used a telephoto lens most of the time. As the sun began to rise, the various tints of colour gradually appeared and changed the intriguing scenes. The Indians greet the sun by lighting a fire in a pit. They live in little mud huts just like the Eskimos' snow huts, and despite the heat they wear multicoloured clothing. As for their dancing, they dressed up in the most gaudy coloured feathers which are overwhelmingly fascinating. This area is miles from civilization and a hundred miles from the nearest telephone or doctor.

Monument Valley, the "living desert" of Walt Disney's film, will never slip from our memory, with its fantastic rock formations made by God and nature. It was fun to live amongst the Indians and film and photograph them way out in the bush. In fact, we shot two thousand feet of 16-mm. colour film to make this Red Indian film. A great privilege to be trusted by this strange race, who have suf-

fered so much at the hands of the white man! Soon they
will be rich, for there is uranium in this district of the
Indian reserve.

We drove on sandy tracks through the Painted Desert
and the Petrified Forest to a town called Flagstaff. This
area is roughly three quarters of the way across America
from New York. Here everyone strolled around in huge
cowboy hats, check skirts, engraved leather belts, tight
drain-pipe trousers, and half-length Indian leather riding
boots with cutaway heels. Guns stuck out of their holsters,
and they looked for all the world as if they were in fancy
dress. In point of fact, some of them were—for only a few
were the genuine article. We could hardly believe our
eyes when we saw every Tom, Dick, and Harry in huge
wide-brimmed hats and cowboy clothes. Everywhere
swarthy-looking Townee Indians walked up and down, for-
bidden to enter a bar or buy at a liquor locker, and yet
many were a bit drunk and potential troublemakers.

We were glad of a bath in the motel and pulled out the
next day through more of the Painted Desert, with its un-
ending wastes of coloured mounds made up of some age-
less volcanic debris. We were glad to have been able to see
and film this desert and the Petrified Forest. This is not a
forest in the true sense of the word, for all around are un-
explained fallen tree trunks turned to stone and lying on
the barren wasteland. The tree trunks were complete with
their bark, which we were able to break off, and yet it was
stone. Some of the stone trees were wonderfully coloured,
due to the various kinds of minerals—copper, sulphur and
the like—which had impregnated the water which had
turned the wood to stone thousands of years ago. Why the
trees are lying on the surface in their original shape and
not under the ground is really quite a mystery.

Already our car was filling up with stones and coloured
rocks which I had been collecting for our garden at home.

Many times we wished we could transport the multi-flowering cacti! The Rockies and the deserts are a paradise for anyone interested in a variety of rocks.

"Oh no, not another one," my wife would say. "How on earth are we going to get them all home? We look like a travelling circus as it is!"

With a guilty look I would smuggle more aboard the car, including gold ore, uranium, and glistening rocks which would glow with many colours if we could one day train an ultraviolet-ray lamp on them.

At last we reached the Grand Canyon, and were rather disappointed with its dull grey, dried-up mud and heavy blue mist hanging over it. We stayed in the wooden hotel on the edge of the south rim of the canyon and felt we were part of millions of American tourists with their cameras and picture postcards. "Just a moment, please, would you mind moving out of the way? I want to take a picture of my girl friend and the view." So we moved from place to place to get out of the way.

The land for very many miles around the Grand Canyon is quite flat. Millions of years ago the earth here split apart, and now the Colorado river runs its violent course through the bottom of the canyon. As we stood on the very edge of this vast abyss, it felt as if we were looking right down into the heart of the earth. Incredible to realise that the river tearing its way through the bottom of the canyon was over five thousand feet down. Raising one's head, one's eyes travelled up layer upon layer of mud ledges in all sorts of shapes till at the top the north rim came into view. A vast and awe-inspiring wonder of the world. It reminded me of Our Lord's description of the hereafter: He said to Dives that He could not send Lazarus to comfort him because between the two of them there was a great gulf fixed.

From here we drove north to the most spectacular and

most colourful canyon anywhere in the world, exceeding all our wildest dreams. It is called Bryce Canyon and is like a vast horseshoe well on the side of a mountain. There is a wonderful view in the distance, and then looking down into the canyon it seems as if you are in some fairyland of weird and wonderful shapes and pinnacles in all the colours of the rainbow. It was like looking down on millions of Burmese temples and pagodas, but made out of nature's sandstone. The centuries of sun, wind, and rain have worn away the soft parts of the soil and stone, leaving these fantastic shapes stretching upwards for a thousand or more feet each. Wherever you look, the colours are dazzling, and there are many archways of hard stone with little chipmunks running all over them.

The Divine Architect of the Universe certainly gave rein to some of His creative ability here. If stalactites and stalagmites in underground caves take your breath away, then this Bryce Canyon will hold you spellbound. We humped our cameras in the broiling heat down through the steep Indian paths and trails through the canyon and took the most superb films we have ever taken in all the years of our film-making expeditions. We plan, one day, to turn our colour films of this overwhelming scenery into a devotional movie called *Lift Up Your Hearts*, and already we have recorded the music tracks on tape, with the help of All Saints' Choir in Beverly Hills.

If there is one canyon in which you can lift up your heart to God in praise and awe of His majesty, it is in the neighbouring canyon called Zion. I can well remember my wife saying to me as we walked and paddled in the stream: "How religious you are in this canyon. It seems to have caught your imagination more than all the rest." There we were, surrounded by rocks of towering height, which had been given names taken out of the Bible. I was tremendously impressed—indeed, fascinated—as I gazed up at the

fantastic rock mountain with its vast white face called "The
Great White Throne." I took pictures of it from every angle,
remembering the words of the Book of Revelation about
the Great White Throne:

And I saw a great white throne, and him that sat on it, from
whose face the earth and the heaven fled away; and there was
found no place for them.

And I saw the dead, small and great, stand before God; and
the books were opened: and another book was opened, which
is the book of life: and the dead were judged out of those
things which were written in the books, according to their
works.

And the sea gave up the dead which were in it; and death
and hell delivered up the dead which were in them: and they
were judged every man according to their works.

And death and hell were cast into the lake of fire. This is
the second death.

And whosoever was not found written in the book of life was
cast into the lake of fire.

REV. 20:11–15

As we sat and looked at that rock with its frame of vivid
blue sky and lovely surroundings, we felt in our bones
something of the majesty of God. We looked from there to
the "Cathedral" rock—a monument to God by God, so much
more majestic than any church or cathedral that man has
ever made. Zion Canyon was so utterly different from any
other canyon, with its wonderful flowers and foliage. Could
anyone walk in Bryce or Zion canyons without feeling that
"the heavens declare the glory of God and the firmament
sheweth His handiwork"? We find a designing, overruling
mind in the world of nature, and we give these attributes
to the creating force, God. We find beauty, colour, music,
and rhythm, and we give these things to Him. How could
there be thought without a thinker; life without a life-

giver; love without a lover? The Peace of God certainly could pass man's understanding here in Zion.

Often, as my wife and I walked together hand in hand, I would recite these lovely old phrases from the Psalms and the Book of Revelation, and then we would smile, draw close to one another, and I am sure God could understand our thoughts. Happy? Of course we were, deliriously so, despite the grim gnawing pains within. God was so very close, and we were thrilled to have each other amid such evident examples of His majestic creation.

At the top of that canyon there is a vast rock called the "Weeping Rock." You can stand in a hollow underneath, and look out through a curtain of tears down the whole length of the canyon. How true it is of life that amidst all the grandeur and all the wonders that you and I can grasp, seek after, and attain, there are things that make us weep. As we look back in our lives, there have been weeping rocks for each one of us. I do not mean rocks of self-pity, for they are the greatest destroyers of human happiness.

As I look back on my life, there have been some weeping rocks, and two stand out in my mind. The first had no tears except those of bitterness, and it was in the first year of my marriage when I was twenty-six, but it taught me how to help others. The second was a very moving and tearful occasion when I retired as Vicar of Holy Trinity, Aylesbury.

After some years of indecision, and with increasing pains inside owing to haemorrhoids and a return of duodenal-ulcer trouble—little knowing what this was leading up to—I wrote thus to my bishop, who had always been a good friend to me:

For the past two years I have been in a great state of in-decision as to whether it is fair to go on running two jobs, or as you once said to me 'riding two or three horses'. Now that the work I have striven for through Dawn Trust is a success, it seems to demand even more time, despite a large full-time

staff drawn from the parish. I have discussed this problem with
a number of bishop friends of mine, like the late Dr Lunt and
Clifford Martin of Liverpool, but it seems no one can decide
matters for another's life.

My health has suffered as one has worked a seven-day week
and burnt the candle both ends, and now I am told that my
duodenal ulcer condition makes it necessary for me to make
up my mind. Not that one puts a deal of stock on doctors!

I therefore have decided to resign my living here at or about
Easter and thus be able to hand on to another a really 'live'
going concern with a full church and very lovable people. It
is done with such a heavy heart. It seems a good thing to give
due notice. I have been told that I must rest a bit anyway,
and it would not be fair to rest 'on' a parish. Thus I propose
to become a paid official of my Dawn Trust and devote say
five years to putting it really on its legs and teaching people
how to use visual aids, and making more.

I shall miss my own altar and my own pulpit and my own
people.

I hope that this decision is thought by you to be a right one
and that I would enjoy a licence to preach in the diocese if I
should ask for one.

This is not an easy letter to write, nor an easy subject. I only
came to my final decision yesterday in that I felt something
ought to be said at Christmas time and since I am supposed to
rest a little time after Christmas.

Looking forward to hearing from you.

I will admit I cried like a child as I took the midnight
Communion on that Christmas Eve, and the memory of it
lives with me as if it was only yesterday. The church had
meant so much to me, and I had taken it over empty at
such a tender age thirteen years before. During the war
years we were flooded with evacuees from London and had
to hold two services on Sunday nights to cope with the
crowds. We had almost rebuilt the church inside, and it

had become like flesh and blood to me. The church had an atmosphere of prayer and mystical worship, and its pulpit was one of those easy places from which to preach and unleash what was burning in one's heart all the week.

This church was Zion Canyon to me, and on that Christmas Eve, when the only light was from the candles on the Christmas tree in the Children's Corner and on the altar, there was a heartbreaking magic in the air. My weeping rock came with those lovely words "Take and eat . . . drink this in remembrance of Me." To say goodbye to one dear person is hard, but, as every parish priest knows, it brings a lump in your throat to say goodbye to your own little flock and altar. Although I was giving them six months' warning, the tears had to come, and the bishop's (Dr. Kirk's) reply was understanding as always:

My dear Vicar,

I was not altogether surprised by your letter. With the remarkable growth of the Dawn Trust I have been wondering for some time whether you would not be brought to the conclusion that you were overworking, and I was rather expecting that if you reached a conviction on this point, you would feel that your distinctive contribution to the life of the Church of England lay more in the direction of films than parochial work.

But I know very well how greatly you will be missed by your congregation at Walton (Aylesbury). Of course, the vast extension of housing in the parish produces new problems, and I am certain you are right in thinking that a tired man doing two whole-time men's work could scarcely give of his best in connection with these developments. But I can say very frankly how sorry I am for your sake that you should have been forced to such a difficult decision. Thank you very much indeed for all that you have done for your Church and parish.

I hope your holiday in Italy will be a very delightful one and put a stop to your anxieties about the duodenal ulcer condition.

Obviously you will have to take care of yourself but a holiday abroad and then a change of air at home should do wonders.

Kenneth

I took my rest in Italy and just as I was leaving England my old friend Del Guidice, commonly known as "Del," telephoned me from Rapallo asking me to stay with him. Del was responsible for the production of thirty-two of the best films which came out of the Rank Organisation in its heyday. He started by making *In Which We Serve, The Lamp Still Burns, The Way Ahead,* and all the rest. He quarrelled with the Rank Organisation and made a few films on his own with the Boulting Brothers, who once used to rewind films for me at Elstree before they began their film careers.

I found Del in Italy, a broken and exiled man, but like all impresarios he had talked his way into a comfortable situation on optimistic expectations. He was almost enshrined, as you might say, in the royal suite of the Excelsior Hotel at Rapallo.

I flew there from England in more senses than one, for the Italian air line allowed me to pilot their Dakota over the Alps myself, with the only instruction in broken English: "Don't crash de mountain."

Del, as always, was issuing statements to the press, building castles in the air, in which I was to direct a film on Mary Magdalene one minute and on the Knights of the Holy Roman Empire the next.

Rossellini arrived at the hotel with much handshaking and was equally outspoken to the press while Ingrid Bergman sat in the corner knitting clothes for her expected baby. Peter Ustinov stayed a few nights just to cheer Del up and add a bit of colour.

The whole holiday in Italy was quite a tonic but unfortunately I was ill again in Rome and had to fly back on the next available plane. The months dragged by and at Easter I took my final farewell of a parish I had served for thirteen years; but I still maintain my Dawn Trust office in the town.

This was indeed my weeping rock, but life always moves on and such occasions help one to understand others.

This rock which weeps in Zion is majestic, and yet it knows that from within itself the tears must come. Some have not the heart to cry. I want to live long enough to go back to the weeping rock of Zion and say "Thank You" to God for my present deliverance. I wonder if we are grateful enough to God for all the good things of life while they last. Or whether He looks over our shoulders and says to Himself: "What an ungrateful person, taking all for granted," or: "How dissatisfied, when life is really so good."

As we walked in Zion we had so much to thank God for, and it was like a second honeymoon. It is wonderful to be in love and to know that you mean everything in the world to each other. I am sure that others can catch this happiness from people in love, just as we caught the music of God in our very being as we walked and talked in Zion.

I had a horrible tug at my heart, for the pains at times were almost unbearable, but one could not possibly spoil such a holiday by blurting out one's innermost fears. Was it a premonition of cancer which made the scenery and joy of companionship more beautiful?

Leaving these wonderful places behind us, we sped on through Las Vegas, Death Valley, and the Mojave Desert, with the thermometer recording 135 degrees in the car. It was a long and tiring hop in one day from Las Vegas to Hollywood, and as we approached Los Angeles we passed miles of down-at-heel shanty houses and crawled through sixty miles of smog. Tired though we were, we drove round and round Beverly Hills before going to our apartment, so that my wife could take her first look at the lovely avenues of palm trees and fabulous houses, many of which I had known eight years ago.

What an extraordinary place Hollywood is, built where there was once a desert. There is not space in this book to discuss Hollywood with all its sincerity, its insincerity, its gaiety, its poverty, its striving for success, its make-believe, its overwhelming friendliness. It is a picture of life and people as it is seen nowhere else in the world.

Hollywood is unique and fascinating, like a magnet drawing you back to itself, no matter in what part of the world you are. "Hollywood," when you are away from it, covers the whole area of Los Angeles to the sea at Santa Monica, yet in reality it is only a suburb of the City of Los Angeles—a suburb that has given way to the rich and more noble Beverly Hills.

Hollywood is an atmosphere that gets into your blood when you have lived there and makes you want to go back —back to the whirl of the fast-moving traffic, the heat, the smog, the swimming pools, the supermarkets, the coloured searchlights, the crowded churches, and, above all, the friendly people, rich or poor. They are all hard workers, and determined to enjoy life, even if so many make a mess of it.

The parties around the swimming pools are more amusing and friendly than anywhere in the world. Indeed, they are fantastic affairs, with as many as eight hundred guests on some occasions, complete with a live circus and funny little jesters who let off bangs behind people so that they spill their drinks. Californians have a zest about them, and the film colony brings a touch of internationalism and an air of "we are just about to go places." There is always a new film to be made which is going to break all records, or a script which would prove a sensation if only someone would read it. Success is the thing—so long as you are a success; and to be a success, you have to make a lot of noise.

Death does not enter into the picture at all, except perhaps in the form of suicide as a way out for some frustrated,
disappointed failure.

It is a vast city teeming with life and overflowing with
smart air hostesses who are to be found serving in the shops,
singing in the choirs, or waiting hopefully round the
studios. Don't imagine for one moment that the film colony
dominates this place, for that is far from the truth. Why,
half America seems to want to migrate here to work at
something, and the rich want to come here to enjoy their
riches. Every kind of church flourishes, including the
cranks, but side by side there is a serious moral problem.

Some say: "Oh yes, Americans give you a wonderful welcome and hospitality, but as soon as you are gone they
forget you for the next guy." That is not true. For eight
years I have corresponded with people I met in Hollywood
way back in 1946, and the moment we arrived the doors
flew open and we began again where we left off eight years
ago, only more mature. They even remembered sermons
and expressions which I had long since forgotten.

I was made an honorary member of the New York Yacht
Club by John Nicholas Brown, as well as of the Los Angeles
Yacht Club and of the Santa Barbara Yacht Club. Thus I
am able to enjoy not just the fellowship of Church and film
people but of those who love the way of a boat at sea.
There is a comradeship amongst sailing people the world
over which has none of the artificiality of social groups.

America, to us, is a vivid encounter and an exhilarating
experience.

CHAPTER 2

One Dreadful Moment

FOR three or four years, as gnawing pains grew inside me, I filled my life more and more with a tornado of work. For years I had done two jobs—pioneering religious films and vicar of a parish of twenty-two thousand people. I enjoy preaching and conducting a service with an appreciative, full congregation. This is more spiritually thrilling than acting can be, though the actor admittedly knows when his work is appreciated. In actual fact, he is only a puppet, speaking lines which someone else wrote and doing things he is told to do. Very few think to tell a preacher that they approve of his efforts, let alone find them a help. How little do people realise that an expression of appreciation along the right lines might turn an obscure minister into a great preacher.

Contact with everyday people is the making of a preacher. Suffering can bring him down to hard earth, and the congregation can feel in their bones that what is said is not all theory.

The parson has to feel and believe sincerely what he is trying to put over. His sincerity springs from the fact that what he is doing is not for money or applause, but for God and to help people.

Such spiritual satisfaction as I have experienced is a help when you are suffering, but hard work takes your mind off yourself. So, for the last three or four years before leaving for America, my tornado of work increased, and just before I left I was conducting film missions in many churches from autumn till Easter with the film *I Beheld His Glory*.

I did go to two British doctors about my pains, but all they said was: "You are overdoing it as usual and must slow up." I asked what the lumps were and I specifically asked if it was cancer and was told not to be ridiculous. "Just a few haemorrhoids, old boy." Many know that experience of going to a doctor and not wanting to bore him or to sound like a hypochondriac.

I tried not to let my wife know; and perhaps she blames me now that I did not tell her more, but if you are ill, you do not like to complain.

I would ache in the night, lie on the floor until I had the strength to get back into bed. I had a schedule to keep to, a job to do, preaching to get through.

When I got to America, I knew it was getting worse and I said: "I can't possibly afford to go to a doctor in America —we haven't got enough dollars." We had to live very carefully to make our dollars last.

Only a few days before I collapsed, I said to my wife: "Even if I feel better in a few days, will you make me go to a proper doctor when we get back to England, just to see what it is all about?"

Anyway, I was determined not to allow these pains to spoil the most wonderful trip across America, or my work. I told myself that others have a cross to bear and life cannot stay still. I remember a poor woman in Vienna, in trouble, begging me to smuggle her through the Iron Curtain in the boot of my car. My wife and I had gone to Vienna as guests of the British Army in 1951 with special passes through the Russian zone to preach in the Garrison Chapel in Maria Theresa's Palace. This woman had her cross to bear as a British woman married to a Czech collaborator with the

Russians. The awful thing was that we got lost in the Russian zone getting out and had some anxious moments till we crossed the frontier sixty miles on.

Before I had left London for America, a friend had given me the name of a cancer specialist in Pasadena, California, pleading with me to go and see him. But I was anxious that no one whom I met should know I was ill.

Three months after our arrival in the U.S.A. I was asked to preach in Tyler, Texas. I was flown there and back from Los Angeles to preach two sermons. I stayed four days and made many friends, for Texan folk are wonderful. One millionaire gave me a thousand-dollar cheque for my religious-film organisation after the Sunday service. Despite constant haemorrhages I did a series of radio programmes and recordings right off the cuff . . . about eighteen in all. Luckily for me the broadcasting studios were in my hotel.

The temperature was 106 degrees in the shade, and one day I watched a man frying eggs on the hot pavement in Dallas and take bets as to how long they would take to cook. I asked one of the onlookers why he carried a gun in a huge holster round his waist. He turned and slowly looked me up and down as if I were a man from Mars. Moving his hand to the gun he said in a slow Texan drawl, "Just to protect myself, Brother."

I wasn't too happy continuing the conversation, so I went into a big drugstore and started buying presents for my family. Just as I was about to pay, the manager walked up, took my bill away and cut it by 25 per cent. When I asked why, he pointed to my clerical collar and said: "Didn't you know that the clergy in America get half price on the railway and a reduction in some shops?"

Americans are so much more religious than the British, and they do not mind admitting it, and talk happily about God. British Christians suffer from an inferiority complex and are so shy about God that they never mention Him.

You can work with a fellow for ten years in Britain and not know if he has any belief or church membership. How different in America—they tell you in two minutes what church they belong to, and they certainly support it.

When many British think this American religion is hot air, they are so wrong. In America, all the churches are overflowing, and those who go, or who are members, support them enthusiastically in cash and loyalty up to the hilt. Church membership is much more a family-unit affair than one of stray individuals, and thus there is a need for a greater stress on the personal conversion of *every* member of the family. There is a great need for reveille preaching missions to create convinced Christians in head as well as heart and in personal conviction. It would be awful for America if a swing against church-going occurred and left many high and dry without definite concrete beliefs. So many of the films, plays, and television or radio dramas are just the cloak of good Christian living without much spiritual core or basis. A vast religious revival is nationwide, but it must be made to go deep into the heart of the individual.

The church I was preaching at in Tyler, Texas, was Marvin Methodist Church and they put on a farewell supper which was attended by about two hundred people on the Wednesday night. I had great fun telling them about England and showing a series of colour films I had made about Britain, Europe, and sailing. They were four busy days with such friendly hospitality. Little did I know that this supper was nearly my farewell to life, for the flight back to Los Angeles was agony.

My wife and I rushed from the airport to find a doctor— the traffic, as usual, was terrific along the fast Hollywood Freeway to Arroyo Seco and on to that lavish township of Pasadena. Luckily, the doctor I wanted to see was in, and when I sent forward the name of our mutual American friend in London who was an evangelist, he saw me at once. "I was told in London," I said, "that I must come and see you if I ever got to America, for our old friend was convinced you could diagnose my pains. He knew I was afraid it was cancer. I've been too busy to come and see you. I have been working on a film out here, and you know what studio hours are. Now I'm all in, as you can see. After a struggle we remembered your name and I looked you up in the phone book."

The specialist had that wonderful gift of making a patient feel that he has his undivided attention, despite the crowded waiting room. "Lost much blood lately?" he asked me as he busied himself with the notes.

"Yes, and during the last few days while I have been in Texas it has been getting worse."

Presently, armed with cards, I passed into the various rooms of his clinic, which was like a minor hospital, where white-coated chemists, radiologists, and nurses went to and fro.

I was X-rayed with newfangled instruments almost all over, and while waiting they took every conceivable test, including a blood-rate test. How long I dozed off in one of the little cubicles, I do not know, but an hour or two later I emerged and had my first physical examination by the doctor. Laboriously he went through the usual routine with more care than I had ever received before.

Finally, with instruments, he examined the rectum, and I was too tired and dopey to ask the question I had asked in London: "Is it cancer?" Not that I was afraid he would laugh me to scorn, as the London doctor did, but because I knew by instinct that he was shocked by that same old obstruction, which was so much bigger now.

"It is like a red-hot poker, or as if rats are gnawing away, and I am so tired," I said.

His couch was so comfortable I longed to sink down in

it and be left alone to sleep. I felt I was in good hands, and I wanted to relax for a long time.

He covered me over and sat beside me and ruffled the back of my head in silence for a bit. "I've read of your mission work in London, but you've got to think of yourself right now, young feller."

"I'm so tired, so very tired." I was indeed tired, too much so; and the more I relaxed, the responsibility of my troubles unconsciously on his hands, the more tired I felt.

"I'm afraid it is pretty serious, young feller. How old are you, again?"

"Almost forty-five, and life has been good but full of struggles."

"Well, I am afraid it is serious now. Too serious to start worrying about fees. I want you to get up and go right away and see some specialists. Dress while I call them up right away to fix the appointment for two-thirty. They are a group of experts."

His tone first shook me from my sleepiness and then made me concentrate on the coming opinions of the experts. Obviously he was not going to commit himself, and he just handed my wife a card and the directions. "Get him there as quickly as you can. They will all be waiting for him by the time you get into Los Angeles."

As she drove me back to Los Angeles in that lovely car, I was concerned about her not getting any lunch, and yet she couldn't care less about lunch. Funny how you talk of mundane things in the very middle of a crisis. We were a team, the two of us: we would chatter as we drove across Europe or America, or we would remain silent for hours, often thinking the same thoughts at the same time.

This time, we drove on in a state of daze; each was too absorbed in personal thoughts and forebodings.

There were two or three specialists and a leading surgeon assembled behind me as the V-shaped table was raised upwards, like a dentist's chair in reverse. Upside down and looking under the table, I found myself staring at their shoes and wondering in a dizzy sort of dream at their beautiful shine despite the heat and dust of Los Angeles. They worked and talked in medical terms which sounded more like a foreign language to me, and they seemed excited at what they saw. I gave up trying to listen, for the blood pressure was building up in my head in this position.

"Has anyone examined you here before in the last eighteen months to five years?" boomed a voice far above me.

In a voice that hardly seemed my own, I replied:

"Four or five years ago, I think it was, the lumps began, and occasional bleeding—just as I was retiring, owing to ill-health, from being Vicar of Aylesbury in England—I am a parson, did you know?" As if it mattered two hoots now who I was in this funny position. "It has got worse lately —lots of pain and utter exhaustion, but I lead a very busy life with no time to rest up."

"I asked if you had ever seen a doctor about it?"

"Why, yes, only a few months ago just before leaving for America. I was in such pain that I went to a doctor in London. He examined me there with his hands, and I asked him what those lumps were and if it was cancer. He laughed and said: 'Of course not. Everyone thinks they have got cancer at the slightest pain. Just a few piles, old boy. You have been overworking, that's your trouble. Take it easy and I will give you some ointment.'"

At that the doctors behind me nearly exploded with anger.

"You mean a doctor saw this and did nothing, and let you come out here to tour America—he must have been crazy, stark crazy. You're sure he was a qualified man?" the senior one asked.

"Of course I'm sure. Look here, will you please tell me

frankly what you have found—the best or the worst. I want the truth, for I have a wife, two lovely children, and a passionate life's work half completed and no money at all, so time is valuable to me." I demanded to be told the cause of their excitement and anger as calmly and coldly as possible. I knew in my very bones just what they would say, and I was shocked, but glad that the reply was blunt and final.

Like a judge proving his point with a lifetime of legal experience behind him, he said: "You have the last and final stages of cancer. It has been growing for years, and clearly visible to any doctor, for many months. Like a large cauliflower, only an inch from the surface, and stretching way up inside. The aperture is more than four fifths of a circle, closed. You've had a lot of pain with this thing over a long time. There is nothing we can do now, kid. Better put your papers in order quick."

"How long will I last?" I asked, as if I were at a train-enquiry office, yet stunned to a state of feeling quite impersonal about it.

"About three days or at the most four—then the passage will be completely closed—may we film it and cut specimens off?"

A few painful minutes passed, for how could I refuse permission to film it if it might help someone else?

"Can't you operate? I need more time. I've made no provision for my wife and children: they'll be destitute."

"Sorry, kid, we wouldn't touch it. It has been left too late. Shall we tell your wife? Can she take it?"

"She is older than she looks," I replied. "Oh, poor darling," I thought as they went to tell her, "what will you do? I wanted us to grow old gracefully together, and now you'll be so lonely. Why did I give all my money to create a nonprofit-making ideal? I should have thought of you.

I've broken my heart to create the Christian film movement and none will rise up to provide for you."

If you can fall down headfirst into a deep well of panic and fear in a split second, this was it. I tried in my mind to climb the walls to get out, but they were dark and greasy. I felt I knew these very walls from nightmares of the past —I had buried so many people during my life and wondered if they were really dead or if they wanted to get out of their coffin just to work a little longer to provide means for those who stood veiled in black behind the coffin.

"Oh, please God—I'm not afraid to die, but I'm terrified for those I leave behind. How will they live and eat? Money, money, money." The noise of my thoughts got louder in my ears and behind my eyes, when suddenly it stopped, and I slipped, unconscious, from my chair to the floor.

Warm arms were round me and her hand on my forehead. I think it helped Catrin to have to help me back to consciousness, for she had the calm and gentleness of a trained nurse, who has learnt to hold her own emotions in check for the task in hand.

"Sorry, darling, I've let you down. Let's go back to our apartment and make the most of these few days," I murmured into a soft warm ear I knew so well.

At that moment I was strangely relieved that it was cancer—relieved that it was all over, the battle for life was at last ending and I could have a long, long sleep. Just what I needed, for a sickening weariness had crept over me and I selfishly forgot this world and the pulsation of life with its work, its love, and its worries, for the sheer pleasure of not having to exert myself any more.

As my wife drove me back along Hollywood Boulevard and Sunset Boulevard to our apartment amid the glare of brightly lighted shops, I felt like a man in a dream. The shops were still open on this Friday night. So long as there were people to buy, they stayed open. Shops which glorified the human body, especially a woman's, glared at you till you were sick to death of seeing advertisements for the upper part of the female form. Does Hollywood ever think of anything else? A one-track mind indeed! They all seemed like puppets in a show, rushing madly about while the going was good.

Yes, that's Hollywood: no time for old age or leisured living. They admit death, but adorn it with skyscraper tombstones, gardens of rest where loved ones are buried in full evening dress and the money paid ensures that a gramophone record plays in the trees near the grave. Music, music, music. Dentists advertise on the radio that you can have your favourite record playing while they take your teeth out—only a few dollars extra. Every Tom, Dick, or Harry turned evangelist blares out on the radio with jazzed-up Jesus songs. Movie makers turn from gangster and sex films to make supercolossal biblical movies in order to cash in on the religious mood of the world. Television advertisers turn to religious behaviour programmes to help sell their commodity.

What a city to die in! Yet for years I've loved it. Its people are so exhilarating, its climate so marvellous, its speed and excitement so terrific.

It all flashed by the window of the car as we sped back to our apartment, overlooking the swimming pool, which was always full of young people with radios blaring and one ear for their telephone bell in the hope that a date would call them up.

At length we slipped to our knees beside the bed to pray as we so often had done, but now it was difficult to find the words.

"Dear God, please forgive me for all the . . ." I began in hardly a whisper, but thoughts rushed in to argue that we must not even hint that we blamed God that cancer

had knocked at my door. "Dear God," I began all over
again, "give me more time to live in this world, more time
to serve You, unworthy though I am to ask. And Catrin
needs me."

"Oh, please God, give me life—I know You can. I'm not
asking for stones to be made bread just for me. But You
have got men who can cure with Your help in one way or
another. . . . Please, I beg of You. I've tried to be brave,
but now I am unwound at Your feet. It is not that I don't
want to meet You—I want to live desperately for her, for
life itself. Oh, it is selfish, I know, but surely there is something I could do for You in this world for those who suffer.
Give me more time, I beg of You. Forgive me for wanting
to die just now: it was selfish and lazy. Oh, God, this cannot be the end."

So I mumbled on, trying to frame every jumbled thought
into words, till I heard Catrin's prayer: "Oh, God, help us
to find the right man."

As ever, the practical woman was right: it was the man
we wanted—we must find God's instrument, and we too
were His instruments.

A new determination or conviction seemed to grip us
both. We must expect God to answer our prayers. It was
no good to go on moaning to Him like this with only three
days to live. "It is lack of faith to go on kneeling here asking
God the same question as if He were deaf," Catrin said. "I
never did agree with people who pray all night and haven't
the guts to believe He heard them the first time. Where's
that telephone book?"

Then began our mad rush against time to locate a doctor
who would be prepared to take a risk and operate. We rang
up various cancer hospitals, but it was now getting late, and
junior interns were the only ones on duty and they were
reluctant to give the names of their big chiefs, let alone
their home telephone numbers.

Friends called and suggested names, those led to other names, and I phoned London for advice.

Of all the surgeons I spoke to on the phone that night, there was one whose voice made me feel I had known him all my life. I liked him, and we rang each other back during the night. First he had to check up with the examining specialists, whom, fortunately, he knew; and he rang back to say, "It's going to be tough going, but we will have a try. Anyway, you'll never make it back to England at the week-end, and you have got a time limit on your head."

When I began to hedge, he read my thoughts like a flash. "Now look here—if you're worried about the fee and the money, I never charge a priest, and least of all a British priest."

I thanked him but said: "That is jolly big of you, yet now it has come to the issue, I want time to think this out and to pray . . . if it is going to be as tough as you say."

Well past midnight I telephoned and said, "Yes, I'll be there in your hospital first thing in the morning, but what about a bed?"

"Good, I knew you would. I've already reserved you a room. Goodnight."

Can you judge a man by his voice on the phone? I think so, but little did we know that this John Howard Payne was a king among surgeons and one who makes great use of the artery bank in modern surgery. (The artery bank is like a deep freeze and the surgeon can now remove an artery from a dead person shortly after death and store till it is needed.) I was convinced that he was to be God's instrument to answer our prayers. He was on the staff of the University of California Hospital and the Good Samaritan Hospital.

My wife telephoned her mother in England to let her know what was to happen, for we felt quite determined that I was going to live. In fact, the whole idea of death seemed too ludicrous to us; but to her mother, being a doctor, the crisis had no ray of hope.

I know God was very close to us as we knelt and committed the night to Him and told Him that we had faith in victory and that I was determined to live.

I had experienced so little sleep in the past few months and I lay awake that night trying to give with the pain because resisting it always makes it worse. Strange, is this business of pain, for there is always a struggle to keep it out of the mind and only in one part of the body. Now that I knew the end was so very near, the difficulty was that while giving with the pain instead of pushing against it I had to gather up the reins of life at the same time lest I should relax and let life itself slip away.

The night seemed to drag on and I occupied my thoughts first with the atmosphere of that modern futurist apartment and then with life as I had known it.

It seemed odd to remember that Judy Garland had filmed in this very room the scenes from her film, *A Star is Born,* only a few months before. The music from a gramophone warbled in through the open windows. How inconsiderate to play a gramophone in the middle of the night, but perhaps it was more melodious than the grinding noise of someone turning on their electric garbage-disposal gadget under the sink.

Sometimes, I was grateful for any noise during the night, if only to know that someone somewhere in the building was awake.

I thought of Catrin and wondered if she was awake and what she was thinking as she lay so still on her bed. How often in the few years we have had together, since we were married by my lifelong friend Canon Bryan S. W. Green in St. Martin's Church, Birmingham, have I known exactly what is in her mind. Sometimes I would purposely race ahead to make a remark at a point in the thought train before she reached there, just for the sheer fun of surprising her and hearing her say, "How did you know I was thinking about that?"

One of the pleasures of being married to someone you love is that you can play hide-and-seek together, in the realms of thought and memory. I start a memory by a phrase about a past incident and guess if she will immediately connect the next thing I am thinking of with it. Life consists not only of the enjoyment of it at the time, but the re-living of the memories of its enjoyable moments, of places and people encountered.

I thought back, of our love. We had meant more to each other than life itself and I was glad that we had never held back one single corner of our lives from each other. I thanked God for the wonder of the love of a true woman and all the refreshing happiness which had never grown stale. A happy marriage of two people hopelessly in love and with common interests and tastes is like a priceless treasure box into which they can constantly dip for new experiences.

My contented thoughts made it all the harder to see the lid of that treasure box close. For me there was pain at the heart of our love now, for if I died she would have to live in this world with only a memory treasure chest while I would be at rest.

St. Paul once said he had a desire to depart because he was convinced there was a better place. I found myself arguing inside, during the night, whether to die was "far better" because there was to be no marriage or giving in marriage so I could not take with me the kind of love-happiness which had meant so much to me. There seemed to me to be no clear answer except the dogmas of theology and I was grateful when the morning came.

When my surgeon walked into my private room, he was far bigger in every way than I had imagined him. A big, thickset man in his thirties, I guess, with a sizzling personality of good humour and friendship. There are some people you click with the moment you clap eyes on them, as if your eyes and personality have been talking to each other for years.

He was fun, great fun, and obviously knew his stuff and was worshipped by the hospital staff in that way hospitals have for their prize men. There was no pomp or secrecy, and what he saw inside seemed to be a challenge to him. "The specialist certainly was right: this is going to be a tough one." He sat down on the bed and began to explain just what he was going to do, and the risks involved.

"First, you and all your many friends here have got to pray, for we both need help with a job like this. Then on Monday morning, starting at 7 or 8 A.M., I will do my part. From the front and then from the back, I will cut out everything that is humanly possible, leaving you just enough innards to enable you to live. Fair?

"We will be leaving nothing to chance lest we miss one single cell. Yes, you will have a colostomy which means that we bring the digestive tract to the surface between muscles, just below the waistline and we will sew you up permanently at the back. So, if I do my part, you have got to do yours. You have just got to be determined to live—no half measures, just one almighty effort."

I promised to do my part and asked: "If it is a success, how long before I can leave for England?" With a grin, he said that it might be about four weeks. I didn't like the twinkle, but at least he promised to send a Britisher back to England alive!

"Now this colostomy—will I always have it if I get through the operation?"

"Yes, I'm afraid it will be permanent and will require an awful lot of patience and mental discipline and adjustment. But you will get by."

So he went off for a week-end's golf, leaving me with his special nurse for the rest of my time.

To punctuate my determination to live, I booked, over the phone, our return plane to London, giving the date as four weeks and four days from the Monday.

Next, I sent a cable to a friend to buy for me and my Dawn Trust a house called "Greystoke," overlooking the sea and Poole Harbour on Canford Cliffs, Bournemouth.

I cabled: "Determined to survive major cancer operation Monday. Buy Greystoke immediately."

I had been offered this fabulous mansion with its graceful blue swimming pool before I left England, but the price then was prohibitive. Only a few days before, I had a cable quoting for the whole place a figure which was reasonable. My dream was to turn this glorious place into Dawn Trust's headquarters and into a top-level conference house—Christian Rendezvous. Neither Dawn Trust nor I had any money, and in fact I had no idea how to raise the purchase-price money. But if I was to live—determined to live—then Greystoke was a big enough target. Maybe it was an emotional decision, but I had to prove my desire to live and my belief that God would guide the surgeon and give me back borrowed time to live and wear His shoes in His service.

It seemed to me an ironical situation because I had planned some provision for my family in the event of just such an emergency as this. A friend of mine from undergraduate days, Wing Commander John Barnes, had arranged a new life-insurance policy for me a few days before I left for America. My London doctor had given me the all clear certificate as being completely fit but John could not accept this on behalf of his Sun Life Insurance Company of Canada although I had already signed the papers. He arranged for me to have a medical check-up by his company's doctor at Southampton just before boarding the

Queen Elizabeth. Unfortunately our car broke down thirty miles from Southampton and we only caught the *Queen Elizabeth* by the skin of our teeth, arriving there in a workman's truck. We missed the appointment and I said to myself, "Oh well, nothing will happen to me in four months."

CHAPTER 3

The Surgeon's Knife

ALL day Sunday we prayed and talked and knew that many in the churches were praying as well; and that night in her own room my wife, as she prayed, had a strange experience—almost a vision of confidence. She feels that this was due not just to her prayers but to the community of prayers at that time, so much so that she slept like a top that night and arrived bright and early at the hospital.

I was sitting up in bed in a back-to-front nightshirt, feeling jolly hungry and talking to London on the telephone. Already the room was beginning to bristle with contraptions which were to be part of my life for some weeks. John—my surgeon—popped in to give us a breezy hullo, as if we were about to raise our mainsail, loose our moorings and put to sea for a week-end cruise. We were already on Christian name terms: it just works that way in America.

They gave me a shot in the arm, but it did not have the slightest effect. I had warned them, but they did not believe me: they were soon to learn how tough I was as far as drugs were concerned. I had just received the most exciting telegram from England as they put me on the trolley, which was enough to stimulate anyone.

My wife and two girl friends retired to spend the whole day in the hospital chapel, while I was trundled off to the theatre along endless corridors and in super lifts. Everything was slick, streamlined and beflowered—just like a Dr. Kildare movie. "Hullo there: are you still awake?" called the floor sister, beaming from ear to ear, as we swept down the corridor.

"Can't miss the show, you know. I'll be back and tell you all about it," I called—for after all, you are allowed to flirt with a sister when you are tied to a trolley.

The operating theatre was a buzz of activity, with white-coated figures coming and going with trays of instruments and chrome cylinders of bandages. This was familiar ground to me, for up at Cambridge, apart from getting a degree in History, I also did a shortened medical course. This involved doing anatomy and physiology and attending operations. I had an idea, once, of being a missionary, and took this medical course in case it might come in useful. In the vacations I had worked as a "dresser" in a London slum medical clinic run by a missionary doctor.

John walked in looking like a member of the Ku Klux Klan, with a highly efficient air and looking disgustingly healthy. He began to talk to his assistants and a pretty girl surgeon, whom I later learned came from Germany.

My arm was stretched out to the right for the anaesthetist to pump the drugs into my veins. I knew there were to be two stages of this anaesthesia, both pretty deep, and therein lay the danger. After they had done the first major operation from the front, they would be turning me over to commence the operation from the back. For this, they really would have to put me under, and it is this and the cutting with the knife which is the touch-and-go moment for the body.

I twitched my fingers, opened my eyes, and kept up a running conversation lest they should think I was "off" and start cutting me up!

"When is this fellow going out? It's up to eight already," said the young anaesthetist. I looked across at John, but could now see nothing but his eyes, for the gauze over his mouth covered up any expression.

I tried to think of Greystoke and past events, but nothing seemed to stay in my mind for long. The old-fashioned ether with a bag over your mouth used to make me feel as if I was in an engine room with a pneumatic drill banging into a long corridor of my brain, getting louder and louder in rhythmic, noisy blows.

This was different: my legs began to draw out a bit long —until I felt about eight feet long—and my arm was going numb. I lost consciousness while mumbling, "I'm not off yet—so don't start."

They worked nonstop for six or more hours, with that meticulous routine of an operating theatre, and first they made a long central incision to the left of an old one. As they went down layer after layer, little clipper pinchers were put on all the severed blood vessels and tissue before they removed for examination the thirty-two feet of intestine.

Then they turned me over and increased the depth of the anaesthetic before they removed everything from the back, leaving only a small opening which has to be kept open for many weeks to allow the whole area to drain and so heal from within the deep parts.

They found the cancer had indeed travelled far further then had been expected, so the rectosigmoid and part of the colon were removed, as well as dozens of yards of lymphatic channels. They next found they had to remove the walls of the pelvis, right down to the very pelvis bones. This was to make me very sore inside for a long time, and a bit painful for walking. These sections were whisked out of the theatre to the laboratory for testing, and it was subsequently proved that John had been cautious enough to remove two inches more than contained cancer. Metastasis had begun in the first node, so apart from the closure, the cancer crab had begun to spread its tentacles beyond the primary growth.

The heat outside was the usual 97 degrees in the shade, but the theatre was air conditioned at the right temperature for operating. Despite this the heat for those taking part behind masks and gloved hands added to the strain.

Blood transfusions were put in before I was wheeled from the theatre and were repeated in my room. This was normally a £1,200 operation, and my surgeon had made no charge and made me feel he was really pleased to do it!

I came round to consciousness a little light-headed and surrounded by strange contraptions. The first thing I remember was my wife's face close to mine and her whisper: "Thank God—it's been a great success. John Payne is coming in to see you in a minute to say it is just as well he did the operation today, and it is going to be O.K."

I do not think many people feel very much pain at first after they regain consciousness, and it is usually sickness which worries them. The little tube they had put down my nostril into my stomach removed all sickness, so life was not too bad! The relapse was probably the worse part, when I kept complaining about my head feeling like cracking open. Frantically they played about with every known drug to bring down my temperature, but my head was too bad to notice the worried faces all around me.

When I heard talk of cancelling the plane booking, I came round from my faraway deep valley to threaten dire consequences if they pounced now and dared to cancel that plane.

"I'll be all right in a day or so," I said, "if only you will cure this headache. I'll present my body for cartage to the airport on the appointed day and if there is no plane I'll be mighty angry. I will do my part and I'll be there, so watch out."

I had no idea how serious the high temperature and the

general situation were till afterwards. Four weeks in hospital had been mentioned merely to soften the blow of all that was to happen to me.

But the result of my tirade was that they did not dare cancel the plane, because they realised I would find out and that it might loosen my determination which was so vital.

I have got over this patch, and everyone looks relieved, but I have to endure the ignominy of my nurse having to deal with my colostomy. I suppose I shall get used to all this in time.

One day someone called who was a really good Samaritan to me. She is a journalist, a foreign correspondent of a famous newspaper, who had heard me preach in St. James' Church, Hollywood, and had been to my press party in our apartment. She was one of the two women who comforted my wife by staying in the chapel with her throughout the operation. Now she came to me and told me that she was a cancer case with a colostomy, and that with a struggle she was making the grade and was thrilled to be alive. Bless her, for her witness is more help to me than all the assurances of the nurses and doctors. Here is someone I can see with my own eyes, walking about gay and happy, even if it was a struggle. Her faith in Christ is stronger than ever, for she needs God so much more now than ever in her life.

Likewise, another ex-colostomy case who was a friend of my doctor has been in to see me. These two will probably never know how much good they have done for my morale. May I do as much for others in my turn one day.

You can hear far more than people think, when you are lying very still in bed, and I overheard someone explaining to my wife that it would cost over three thousand dollars to occupy a private room for four weeks. At this I threatened to get out of bed, tubes and all, and leave the hospital,

but they hushed me down and told me the wonderful news
that it was all paid for by the kind friends who were praying for me.

My very good friend, Mary Pickford, and some of the
clergy had spontaneously started a fund and notified some
of the churches I had visited. We were presented with a
dossier of their names. An example of overwhelming spontaneous kindness, which I think could only happen in
America.

I never thought that my visit to America would end in a
private room of an enormous Los Angeles hospital, with
the walls covered in "Get well" cards from hundreds of
American friends. One is a gorgeous card from the Los
Angeles Yacht Club, inscribed by a host of members, who
seemed to have appreciated a couple of my talks. Another
card is inscribed all over by members of the young people's
group at my beloved All Saints' Church, Beverly Hills. God
bless them all, and I say "Thank You" to God for the love
and affection of this host of friends as I lie here and look
at the array of cards, telegrams, and flowers. The flowers
from Mary Pickford and Raymond Massey outshine all the
rest—film people certainly know how to do these things.

Among the telegrams I have three I read over and over
again to while away the time. The first is from Cuthbert
Bardsley, a bishop in England, who is a wonderful inspiring man and a kindred spirit. The second cable is from my
good friend Spyros Skouras, the head of Twentieth
Century-Fox, who once persuaded me to write a film script
of the life of Jesus in modern English. It took me two years
and was cross-checked by Dorothy Sayers, Professor C. H.
Dodd, and others, but, like so many film projects, it was
put on the shelf. One day I shall publish it as a book entitled *More Than a Prophet*. The third cable is the exciting
one which I received just as I was going into the operation

theatre: "Greystoke yours, Brian. Hurry up and get well. (Signed) Jim."

This cable comes from a yachting friend at home in Dorset who is a director of my Dawn Trust. It is this telegram and the photos of the fabulous mansion called Greystoke on the walls which help to inspire me to get well and to live once again. Greystoke is my dream castle (complete with a swimming pool more beautiful than those at Beverly Hills!); I want to leap out of bed and work hard to make my dream castle come true, and then I will invite all my American friends to come and stay.

But wanting is one thing and leaping is quite another. My special nurse, who never leaves my room all day and arrives horribly early in her own car, says I have got telephonitis and that I am so immune to drugs that they wake me up rather than send me to sleep. She had pretended to be angry when I delayed the trolley taking me to the operating theatre, to talk to my solicitor, who telephoned me from London. He had assured me that my will was in order and that he had recorded that I had appointed my wife chairman of Dawn Trust if I should "snuff out."

I think nurses rather enjoy scolding their pet patients, but this one, Mrs. Florence Carpenter, is the salt of the earth, as so many nurses are. She puts up with an awful lot of teasing and knows just where the pains are and where to rub her hands or inject morphia. If ever a woman worked to give life to her patient, it is she, and we do our morning "surgery" to the accompaniment of my groans and the jazz which pours forth from my midget radio.

"Now turn over thataway, and I will put the ray lamp on you." This word "thataway" causes so much laughter that it helps to break the tension and inevitably my surgeon, who comes to see me every day, arrives at this moment and increases the laughter. But do not imagine that it is all laughter, for there are an awful lot of tears. At

times when my wife, John, and my nurse are in the room
it is quite like a family party!

Having been a patient in a number of British hospitals,
as well as chaplain of an eleven-hundred-bed hospital, I
think I worried about the probability of an uncomfortable
bed almost more than the operation itself. But the bed is a
beauty and can be fixed at any angle so that I can see out
over Hollywood at night, see its bright lights, and its
coloured searchlights in the sky and hear the roar of cars
and police sirens on the Freeways.

Apparently I woke up during the night, after my seven-
hour double operation, to the irritating click of knitting
needles, and promptly ordered the night nurse out of the
room. I am told that my demands were accompanied by
threats that I would ring the police if she did not go. This
running battle went on for a few days until I won, and now
I am trusted to be left alone at night except for those who
pop in every hour. I managed to unthaw the night sister
so that I can get anything out of her, from drugs to hot
milk and hot-water bottles. She will even stay and talk for
hours in the night when I cannot sleep, and she does not
scold me for working with this tape recorder.

The only thing that really annoys me and even sends me
to sleep is the television set in the corner. How people can
bear these constant advertisements, old-fashioned British
movies and out-of-date Wild Westerns, I just do not know.

A hospital is a world all to itself, and it is strange how
important every detail is to the patient.

How grateful I am to a private all-night male orderly
who comes to visit me during the night: he is more gentle
than any woman when he adjusts my tubes. His name is
Ruben and he is, I think, a Jewish refugee from Poland. In
this hospital he is getting danger money. A heavily insured
labourer patient had been hit on the head by a crane and
had part of his brains bashed in. His insurance firm paid

for the best medical care for the rest of his life. Brain specialists keep him alive, but at times he fights like a tiger; and poor Ruben came to my room one evening with two black eyes and bite marks on the arms.

Among other good deeds that Ruben performs is his taking my tape-recorded talks to a cripple boy at his digs who can never go out, and so through this dedicated male nurse I am able to talk and encourage someone else in trouble.

But now I must get away from the confines of my room and all the contraptions which hang round my bed, to talk about the struggle to hang on to faith in Christ in the face of the challenge of cancer. I flick the pages of my Bible over and my eye catches the well-marked passages and scribbled notes. But the print dances before my eyes and a mist of tiredness blots it out, so I have switched off the light and all that is left is the glow of the magnetic eye of the tape recorder.

In the darkness I am trying to think out loud about prayer, the mystery of suffering, the need for a balanced spiritual view, Christian fellowship, doing good—oh, so many things, but will there be time to put into words all I want to say . . . ?

CHAPTER 4

Does Praying Do Any Good?

JUST before I was going in for my operation, two very dear friends of mine in Los Angeles came into my room. One was the Dean of St. Paul's Cathedral, David del Scovil, and the other, the Rector of All Saints', Beverly Hills, Jack Smith.

In New Testament fashion, they laid their hands upon my head and prayed that God's blessing would rest on me as I went through the operation and preserve me in life that I might give more service to Him in the years to come. My wife joined them in their prayers. I knew that with their prayers and with their hands went the prayers of the congregations where I had preached in America, for they had sent cables on the Saturday to those churches asking them to pray. They were representatives of all my Christian friends, of the Church of England and the mission fields, some of whom under the guidance of God I had brought to a knowledge of Christ.

I was grateful for their prayers, and I believed that God would work, because He had said that where two or three are gathered together in His name, He would grant their requests. I knew that even if, for some reason which we with our human minds could not see, this was to be the end for me, it was still right to trust God, and it would not counteract the prayers that they prayed for me.

I want to write now about praying. As I talk into my tape recorder by my bed, it is the middle of the night—one of those nights when you cannot sleep, when every ache in your body comes alive, when you desperately long for the gift of sleep. Many suffer from sleeplessness: I have done so for some years and more especially since the cancer pains have really got going.

The subject of praying raises some very difficult problems. I find it awfully hard in church to pray those magnificent prayers for the whole world-wide existence of mankind.

I always "corrupt" those beautiful staid prayers to something in which I can identify myself as I pray them. I know from letters from my congregation that many feel the same. For example, we don't know that God wants a person to live, but we do know that by praying the Spirit of God brings to that person a tender remembrance of our love, our fellowship, and our expectations for him. I am very keen on friends and count them more valuable than possessions. I have friends scattered all over the world and I often regret the distances between us and the infrequency of our meetings.

These are people whom God has given me, and I believe that I should cherish them and should pray for them.

The easiest prayer, the first stage of prayer, is that I should ask God, at the moment of my praying for a loved one, to bring them a reminder of my love and my fellowship for them. At least our faith can believe He can do that.

It is something more than mental telepathy: it is spiritual telepathy. If you have never prayed before, at least you can begin here. When I pray for my wife, I say to God: "O God, bless Catrin at this moment, remind her consciously or unconsciously of my love for her, of the arms I would bear her up in, of the tenderness I would give her, the strength I would love to impart. Give her this remembrance, this consciousness by Your presence. Within You she is safe, that in us two she is not lonely. Please, God, grant this in Jesus' name."

Can you pray for someone else? Can you get as far as praying for someone who is ill? Since you do not know God's will for them, you must not lose faith if your prayer is not answered and they do not recover.

Pray for someone who is sick, asking God to guide the doctors and nurses, to strengthen the spirit of your friend, asking Him to remind him at that moment of you, of all the love you bear that person, all that you wish for him for health and courage. The joint impact of this spiritual telepathy of God and yourself is bound to batten itself on to that person and help to sustain him. We are invoking a mystical, spiritual power.

Let us pray less for *things* and more for the influence of the Spirit of God. Have you heard of a "prayer-wave"? I hope the idea of prayer-waves increases; for it is an idea that the church seeks to encourage. There are many praying circles in the field of missionary work and divine healing.

Many of my friends with one accord and one mind sent out prayer-waves to God asking Him to guide the wonderful surgeon, Dr. John Howard Payne, as he operated, and the nurses as they looked after me. They prayed that He would give me the strength to want to live, to keep my faith unflagging during the battle. I know that those prayers were felt by me and were effective in my personal battle to keep the faith to win. I feel I must not let either God or them down. It is easier to believe in prayer if we ask for spiritual things rather than material things.

When you ask people to pray for you, ask them to pray specifically for these kind of things, for they are within the limit of your belief. Some people pray grandiose prayers—I don't know that I can really enter into them. Some people pray all round the world: "God bless the Indians, bless the so-and-so's, bless the so-and-so's." But so often such prayers become just a matter of meaningless words. Like over-grown children they rattle off the list. You and I have to talk to God about all the little things. God has told us to pray the Lord's Prayer; sometimes I only get halfway through it because my mind, when I am suffering, loses its grip, but God understands, and I take it up again.

If you have little children as I have, pray for them and with them. We have knelt down together so often and prayed, and I think that is the bond which ties my chil-dren to me more than anything else—our prayer time to-gether. I can remember my little girl, when she was very young in her cot, saying: "Now the prayer about the crumbs." She was remembering a prayer from the Com-munion Service called the humble access prayer, which I had adapted to a child's mind.

It is the most lovely prayer, a prayer of humility. It is a prayer, I think, that we should steep into our children and into ourselves. I would lean over her cot and say it, and she mouthed the words with me, with her own funny little imagination about it:

"We do not presume to come to this Thy table, O Merci-ful Lord, trusting in our own righteousness but in Thy manifold and great mercies. We are not worthy so much as to gather up the crumbs under Thy table, but Thou art the same Lord Whose property is always to have mercy. Grant us therefore, Gracious Lord, so to live in this life that we may be counted Christians and that in the world to come we may enter Your Father's House in which You have prepared a room for us. Through Jesus Christ, our Lord." I am sure the child pictured a big black cat under God's table eating up the bits. Teddy was once made to join in the prayer, for I was told: "He often eats crumbs."

Susan loved that prayer, and I love it too. Then my boy when he was small loved his kind of prayers. He liked: "Support us all the day long, Lord, in this troublous life, till the shades lengthen, the evening comes, the busy world is hushed, the fever of life over and our work done. Then, Lord, in Thy mercy, grant to us and those we love, safe lodging, holy rest, and peace at the last. Through Jesus Christ our Lord. Amen."

When Colin was very young, he was a little afraid of the dark. He would like me to pray with him that prayer— "Lighten our darkness, we beseech Thee, O Lord, and by Thy great mercy defend us from all perils and dangers of this night. For the love of Thy only Son, our Saviour, Jesus Christ. Amen." I used to tell him there could be no ghosts where the name of Jesus was mentioned and that he must trust Jesus to look after the night.

Now that is something I want to stress, even to adults, that if you are alone and you are afraid of the forces of evil, you must mention the name of Jesus. Those forces, mark you, are very, very strong: stronger than most people imagine. "We wrestle not against flesh and blood but against principalities, against powers, . . . against spiritual wickedness in high places."

Just beyond bounds of sight and touch are evil forces. If you play with them as some people play with spiritualism, you are playing with something that is more dangerous than the hydrogen bomb. When you feel the forces of evil too near you, surround yourself with prayers to Jesus—remembering that at the name of Jesus every knee shall bow and the devil trembles. Those who are perhaps a bit psychic—tough luck on them—above all people need to pray.

As I lie in bed on this hot, still night, I know that behind the distant roar of traffic and police sirens which goes on all night—behind the myriad twinkly lights and searchlights which I can see from my bed—Evil is walking the streets.

The dominating spirit force and personality of Evil is driving men and women on to commit crimes and to ruin their lives. The momentum of evil latent in our world is indeed frightening when you think about it. When Evil "comes in like a flood" then will "I lift up a standard" against it.

We need God's help. We should always kneel before we fight, we should talk with God and tell Him all about our problems.

Thus prayer is not so much praying for things, but talking to God about things and joining up with the Kingdom of God as co-workers with the Nazarene.

Are you married? Does your husband or your wife believe? If you ever hope to keep the love bond, which is born of God, alive between you, if you want to keep this tenderest of all plants, which so easily withers—then, for goodness' sake, pray together to God. Get God's sunshine on to your joint love in church—don't be afraid to let her hand slip into your hand in God's house. At Aylesbury I had a full church, particularly for Evensong, and I would put the congregation lights out for the lessons, for the prayers and for that second lot of prayers which I would have extemporaneous, and for the sermon. Their attention was riveted first on the altar, essential for Christian worship, and then on the sermon. I hope that many a married couple would have a hand steal into each other's and so enjoy together the balm of God's presence on this tender plant called married love. If you possibly can, get down on your knees together in your own room. I wonder how many, when they have fallen in love, think that they have reached the measure and the depth of their love in this world for another person. Their very presence means everything to each other.

How many times have I married people in my church and as they have come up the aisle and then made their vows before God, they look as if they imagine that this is the crowning day, that they can never love the other person more. And yet, as life goes on, love can deepen. I think that married love takes a real step forward when two people look over the side of the cot of their first-born child. Love takes a very definite step forward to realise that this little human being belongs to both of them.

Surely they would be very unfeeling if they did not vow between them that they would do everything in their power to ensure that that child had the best possible start in life, and then they begin to be more unselfish than they have ever been before. That giddy, ill-adapted girl now begins to toil and work for that child. And he? He is prepared to make sacrifices, to store his money to ensure that the child has the best possible start.

Here, when we come to the end of ourselves and begin to think in this way of another person, we come to the beginning of God, because a little child is very like God. It is very trusting: God trusts us with so much in this world —and how much do we fail Him? We fail Him, we grown-ups, by becoming hard, insincere, callous, and unthinking. But then, when we have the advent of a little child in our home, love can begin all over again and we begin to be unselfish.

It is this kind of thing that I want you to think about at this moment: we will do our very best for that child as it grows up. We must not forget that the very best does not only consist in giving way to it, or giving it clothes or food and seeing that it has the best possible time, but also does really mean that we have got to get to know God a great deal better, because children are awfully shrewd. They know whether we really believe in God, they know if we are sincere, and so we should give more to the thought of God if we ever are going to give that child its best possible start in this world.

I know many parents, who, when they have had a child, have turned to each other and said: "Let's pray for it." It is probably the first time they have ever prayed together, and they fumble the words out loud, chiefly consisting of "O God, bless our little child"—and then they may not ever pray again.

If you are ever worried about keeping your husband or your wife, do not forget that we are met in God and He can keep us together, and so I would suggest that you remind yourself of His love. You remember these words: "Mine is an unchanging love, higher than the heights above, deeper than the depths beneath, free and faithful, strong as death." We should so trust God that we come to trust one another, and especially when He trusts us with the life of another little child in this world.

Remember that a child's basic character is formed between zero and five, and after that there is very little you can do about it, and only the catastrophic conversion of Christ can change it very much. So it means that as you hold your child in your arms, when you are sending it to sleep or to get its windy puffs up, you may be breathing not just an ordinary lullaby, but a spiritual one. I can remember holding my little boy in my arms and singing that old, old chorus I learned as a child: "Over and over, like a mighty sea, flows the love of Jesus, flowing over me." It wasn't sung very well, but when I stopped, he would cry for me to go on! We can breathe into our children the urge that will form their characters as we pray over them. Later on in life, don't just pray together when the good things happen, but pray when horrid things happen. Perhaps I should have said this the other way round? So many people pray only when they are in trouble and it is extraordinary how patient God is with us.

You need to pray. Jesus taught us to pray direct to God as if He were a personal father. I believe what the Bible says: that there is only one mediator between man and God—the man Christ Jesus—and so without waiting till I am perfect I can come direct to Him and tell Him of my troubles.

Lying here in the hospital, I ask Him for sleep; I ask Him for strength; I ask Him that my witness through this book may be a source of comfort and help to some sufferer who may chance to read it. I pray that it may encourage some who have long since ceased to pray, to begin again and talk with God who is right by our side—nearer than hands and feet.

One day I plan to publish a bedside book consisting of all sorts of unorthodox prayers which I have jotted down in my Bible over the years.

When I was in my teens I scribbled into my interleaved Bible three rules:

1. Keep on praying even when you are up against it.
2. Keep on reading your Bible even if you don't feel like it.
3. Above all keep a sense of humour.

Now the sense of humour is most important, for it strikes a balance between the first two and prevents one becoming a crank and overserious. It also stops one being too introspective. You know the kind of people who always say: "I am a failure. It is no good my trying any more to be a Christian." They succumb to spiritual depression. This can become the very precipice of insanity because it leads to too much introspection, which is never healthy.

The mind is such a delicate mechanism and it can so easily be upset if we feed it with dark and dismal thoughts. The mind needs uplifting, especially when it is overstrained from suffering, overwork and the speed of modern life.

The fresh air of God sweeps away the cobwebs in our brains as we talk with Him and quietly meditate in His presence. But do not take the first floatings of the subconscious mind and call them the guidance of God. To be sure of God amid the clutter of our own lives we have to know Him very well indeed.

CHAPTER 5

Mystery

"My God, my God, why hast Thou forsaken me?" Of all the cries of Jesus, this is probably the most mystical of them all. He took it from a verse in the Old Testament, and at that moment of His suffering He repeated it. Those who have really suffered in this world, who have really known what pain is, have again and again taken on their lips, as I have done in moments of stress, those very words: "Eloi, Eloi, lama sabachthani?" (Mark 15:34).

My God, my God, yes, in the midst of our suffering He is still our God, but we cry out in our pain, to know why it is that such crushing pain should afflict us here in this world. There seems to be no answer or reason, and at the moment of the crisis of pain God does seem far away. There seems to be no real answer to pain. It is obvious that God doesn't send it, because He is a God of Love. It's obvious that God doesn't give you exemption from it, so I find that my only prayer can be at this moment of pain, when the hospital corridors are quiet and the night passes on with leaden feet: "My God, my God, don't forsake me, give me Your presence in it, give me Your power to bear it and not to blaspheme against You."

That is where the issue comes—not to curse or blame God because you suffer, because inside you there are pains of body and mind: and only those who have had cancer know what this kind of pain is. Maybe in the years before it was discovered you have known that terrible pain inside and yet have carried on. You have known what it is to cry out in your spirit to God and hate to make a fuss.

It is odd how quickly you forget the details of past sessions of pain, and this is something we must cultivate. But some occasions stand out in one's memory. The Saturday night before preaching at Gracechurch, Colorado Springs, stays out in my mind, for it was spent groaning in the bathroom, trying not to let my wife know of my agony. Next morning, I had to get up and preach the message of Christ. I can remember just what my sermon was—it was Faith. "Forsaking All I Take Him. Feeling Afraid I Trust Him. Finding Another I Tell Him." I wanted to talk to them about pain, but I felt I could not trust myself. A preacher has to inspire and preach with happiness, wit, and good humour at times when inside he feels like death. His strength is made perfect in our weakness. The gift of preaching is a satisfying and relieving thing, and I thank God for this gift.

But now for a moment I want to talk to those who feel a fellowship with me, who know what it is to have a cancer; what it is to go through a big operation; and know how tender life is for days on end in the hospital.

There is the dread, too, of living with a colostomy for the rest of your life, and the dread of wondering how long it will be before the cancer breaks out again. The dread of having your breast removed or a tube in your neck. I am talking to you: and in fellowship with you I ask—will you also, with me, believe that God still is a God of Love? He is, you know, and we can trust Him, we people who have to face this particular disease.

If we don't trust Him, there is very little else left to hang on to in life, because when you boil it all down it is only when you are well that you think that you are big enough of your own stature to face life. Yet how easily you are knocked down and humbled to know how small is your strength and how large is the world you have to face.

As I lie in this funny position with a pipe down my throat I feel so much at the mercy of the elements, and I need God, and in suffering I learn to creep away to God with a different kind of faith—a faith not built merely on theology, but a faith built on the kind of Christ who knows all about me, to whom I say the most ridiculous things. The relationship becomes a living thing, and I would have you, if you are in any suffering, build up within your heart this kind of fellowship, able to lie in bed and rest back on God—to look up at the ceiling and feel not lonely but strangely united to Him.

It is never, never easy; you feel like rebelling, but it is the only thing worth while, it is the only thing to hang on to. Lucky you if you have got another human being to cling on to in this world. My wife comes to see me and stays almost all day. You are lucky if you have a wife, or mother, or children—they can be a help. I know I have many things to be grateful to God for.

Sometimes all these vanish away. Then you must fall back on those things in your life that can be put on the credit side or else you may fall victim to self-pity. And once you fall victim to that, you have no reserve left against pain or suffering or loneliness. If ever I have to face another session of operations, I can only hope that I shall have enough reserve of faith not to give way to self-pity, because I know that then it will be the end. Self-pity breeds defeat. Self-pity is so boring to others and they shun the person concerned.

It is not easy to explain exactly why it is that having this particular illness, which is so greatly feared, does not weaken or destroy faith, but in many ways restrengthens it.

As to operations, you have just got to believe in the power of the human body to get well: but also you have got to have the will to live, an utter determination to live. God helps those who help themselves.

Anybody who has such an operation is always told, as I was, of the great success it is bound to be and of the many others who have been through similar operations and survived. Unfortunately they seldom name any one specific person. It is only natural to wonder whether that is going to be true in your own case. But each one of us has to face realities, however much the doctor may reassure us. We must take ourselves back to God again and say: "I am prepared to go on believing, even if I may die; even if it takes time to get well or if I have to have lots more operations." I cannot say now just what I will feel like in the days to come: no man can prophesy as far as that in the future. But my prayer is not, of course, "Please do not let this happen"; but, "If it shall be, please may I have sufficient of Your Presence to carry me through."

We have, to put it bluntly, got to have spiritual guts and not intellectual furniture. I hope that if you are faced with the same prospect, you will have sufficient of His presence to carry you through—but you must have a consuming desire or will to live, to get out of that hospital, out of that bed and into the stream of life.

Now I said at the beginning that I was not afraid to die, because I trusted Christ. Death is the easiest thing in the world to face! It is not having to face death that we mind: it is the dying that we do not like, or the thought of living in a maimed condition. I do not suppose many of us, if we were once faced with it, would mind "snuffing straight out" and standing before Almighty God, knowing that Christ was there to welcome us. It is this drawn-out business of suffering that none of us like. It is at this point that we have our very deepest need of God, especially when the night is sleepless and the hours of darkness go by so slowly. It is a struggle to conquer fear in order to live. It makes my feet grow cold and it goes right up my body and I find I am trembling and have to tell myself not to be so absurd, and have to argue: "Of what am I afraid? Is it to die, or is it the dying, or is it the desire to live?"

I am sure many prisoners of war would agree. I have a friend, Dr. J. L. Wilson, who is now the Bishop of Birmingham. When he was the Bishop of Singapore he was captured by the Japanese and for six years or so was tortured and made to live under the most terrible conditions. He told me that he reached a point in the suffering when there isn't any more, when all is nearly finished and a sense of triumph creeps in. After all, you can only die once. With Christ it must have been a triumphant cry—"It is finished" —because He had broken through the physical barrier of suffering and knew that the end was a triumph. It is sad to think of those prisoners of war who approached that point of no return of suffering and were never allowed to pass beyond it. Now the bishop could tell you something of his faith in Christ and the way he lived, so don't let us think that we are alone in facing difficulties, and it is for that reason that this little book is being written.

You should never think that you are alone, but above all, that you have in Christ the greatest fellowship and beyond Him the fellowship of all those who have gone before you, who have believed and trusted.

This is part of what is meant in the Apostles' Creed when we say we believe in the "communion of saints." Not that you or I think we are saints, but we believe in Him and we claim the forgiveness of our sins in Him and not in our works.

So, when there is that agonising moment of suffering, there comes around you also a mystical moment of fellowship with all those who believe in Him. Call this angel

presence if you will, call it the result of the prayers of
those who love you and who are praying for you. I don't
know what it is: I think it is a bit of everything, the kind of
fellowship, the kind of help that Christ brings, even when
the soul seems empty.

So it is not always true to say, "My God, my God, why
hast Thou forsaken me?" I am so glad Jesus made His cry:
it helps me, it is like the screech of an owl on a dark, windy,
rainy night. At my cottage by the water's edge on a lonely
peninsula in Poole Harbour, I used to listen to the sea birds
—curlews, redshanks, herons, and cormorants—grubbing
for food in the spartina grass at low tide in the middle of
the night. It is like some weird chorus of music of delighted, hungry, anguished creatures. A mixture of cries
which speak to me of life. So Christ's midnight cry, "My
God, why?" is music to my very soul, and I know *I* am
within His fellowship. I have, as a vicar and Royal Air
Force chaplain, attended many in suffering and in death
and held their hands tightly as they passed over into another world.

Death never ceases to be a mystery to me, but this one
thing about it I know—it is not the end, for life has brought
immortality to life. I have this poem scribbled in my
Bible:

> The pain we have to suffer seems so broad
> Set side by side with this life's narrow span
> We need no greater evidence that God
> Hath some diviner destiny for Man.
>
> He would not allow this life to send
> Such crushing sorrows as pursue us here,
> Unless beyond this fleeting journey's end
> Our chastened spirits found another sphere.
>
> So small this world; so vast its agonies!
> A full life is needed to adjust

These ill-proportioned wide discrepancies
'Tween the Spirit and its frame of dust.

So when my soul writhes in some aching grief
And all my heart-strings tremble at the strain,
My reason lends new courage to belief
And God's hidden purposes seem plain.

CHAPTER 6

Facing Up to Things

How many people go through life with the awful fear hanging over their heads that one day they may develop cancer? If you are afraid of having a finger lanced when it is poisoned, then you are afraid of having cancer. Therefore, somewhere within you, you must build up enough reserve of faith and courage to face life.

How? May I take you first then to the Bible, where Christ said: "Peace I leave with you, My peace I give unto you. Not as the world giveth, give I unto you." Now what is this peace that Christ gives us Christians? It never is the folding of hands, lying down in a deck chair, and being at utter emptiness with the world. It is not exemption from pain, problems, or punishment.

His peace is the possession of adequate resources to meet every need. That is the ideal that we Christians must aim at, in our personal lives and in our personal faith, be we Church of England, Episcopalians, or Methodists, or Presbyterians, or Roman Catholics.

Whatever we may be, the kind of peace we get from Christ after He has forgiven us our sins, after we have made the one important transaction with Him, is the possession of resources sufficient to meet every need. We build these reservoirs of strength through the study and meditation of the Bible, through partaking of the otherworldly mystery of the Sacraments, through fellowship with the good people of God and through hard work.

If you say to yourself, "I can meet every need but cancer," you are not facing the whole problem. If you say, "I can meet every need but a broken home and the loss of someone I think I love, either through infidelity or through death"; if you say you can face "everything else but some one particular thing," then you are not being honest with your faith. Your faith has not gone deep enough, for faith is the possession of adequate resources to meet every need.

When you look at the needs of the world, secular people can provide food, secular people can provide clothing and houses. Only God and His Church can provide the spirit of a man or woman, and courage to face their lot in life.

I want to put as much emphasis as I possibly can on the fact that becoming a Christian is not an insurance policy against all the slings and arrows of outrageous fortune.

Do you remember that St. Paul once wrote: "I reckon that the sufferings of this present time are not worthy to be compared with the glory which shall be revealed in us"? In other words, although Paul was a Christian and a more devoted follower of Jesus than you or I will ever be, he had sufferings in this earthly life. Yet for him "being a Christian" did not give him exemption from all the misfortunes that happen in a world that man has turned upside down. Paul's "thorn in the flesh" is thought to have been blindness, and beside this he was often beaten up physically by the thugs of his generation. God did not make his tent-making trade so prosperous that he could ease up. God did not arrange a smooth passage through life for him, even amid his good works.

We suffer in this world whether we are Christians or whether we are not. We do not, because we become Christians, get any special exemptions from God. So do not listen to the kind of preaching that gives you the idea that if you become a Christian, everything is going to be all right; or that the Lord is going to bless you with a prosperous business so that you become a millionaire, and all the other nonsense.

It is so easy sometimes for millionaires afterwards to say that the Lord blessed them especially, because they "gave their business to the Lord," and that it was God who made them millionaires. They are reading back into their lives what is not true. They certainly have to shoulder the responsibilities and dangers of being rich.

Jesus, the best man who ever lived, went through terrible suffering. Not so much the physical suffering of the Cross, but the suffering that His friends, those He loved, had let Him down.

He was human as well as divine, and in the Garden of Gethsemane He wanted human hearts on whom He could rest and rely, so He took three of them to watch and pray with Him in His hour of temptation, and yet they fell asleep. He knew the cry of human companionship: in the midst of His agony when He knelt before His God and said, "Not my will, but Thine." He prayed that the cup of suffering and all that it meant to Him would pass away from Him—yet all the time not His will.

Then He turned to find the human hearts He had wanted to be there in loyalty and companionship. His friends were asleep, and He made that wonderfully forgiving remark: "The spirit indeed is willing, but the flesh is weak."

Jesus went on to suffer, not the crucifixion only of the body, but the crucifixion of the soul: the knowledge that mankind had risen up and rebelled against God, its maker, and that His very friends had deserted Him. He died, not of physical exhaustion, but of a broken heart. When the soldiers came to break the legs of those who were crucified lest they should run away from the pit when they were taken down from the cross, it so happened that they did not break His legs because the unusual thing was that He was dead already, the others weren't. A soldier thrust a sword or spear into His side and there flowed out blood and water. He died of a broken heart, broken over the sins of humanity, over the agony of the world gone astray from God.

Don't let us forget that in the turmoil of Jesus there was something more than physical suffering. He must have bitten His lip at the imprint of the nails, He must have bitten His lip at the pain of the cross, of the crown of thorns, just as you and I have bitten the sheets in our bouts of pain, lest we cry out. Many, many times in this hospital I have gripped hold of the rail of my cot and felt the hot tears stream down as I bit the pillow and asked God for strength over this ache inside. But God had something bigger to endure. God and Christ had a heart that was yearning over humanity.

Whenever you and I are suffering, when we think that it is bodily suffering that is getting us down, remember that Christ suffered and Christ died for the sins of the whole world. Of course, the tragedy, as you and I know, is that while He died for the sins of the whole world, the whole world is not being saved, the whole world is not turning to Him.

It is our job, if we can, with all the life left to us to bring others into a knowledge of Him, that He may save them and write their names in His book of life.

So I return to the theme of this chapter, which is that being a Christian is not an insurance policy against misfortune.

Suffering may come your way—it did come mine—it has got to be faced. We have got to believe that underneath are His ever-loving arms, and that He gives us the strength to live through it and not an exemption from it. If ever you get the chance to talk to any other Christian, will you try and tell him that? Will you try and tell him that when he is well?

Don't pin your faith on the idea that God has an extra-special dispensation for you, and that's why you believe. You don't believe because He has made you happy, because He has given you a wife who loves you, children you adore, and a home that you can live in and a job that just keeps you going.

All those things make you thank God. By all means thank Him, but don't take them as signs and tokens whereby you believe in Him. Believing in Him goes far deeper than that —it is believing in Him although you have nothing. Do you remember again what Paul said: "I count all things but loss . . . that I may win Christ." In other words, that you and I count all our worldly gains, all the lovely things that we enjoy at God's hands and the hands of others, as nothing compared with the inner peace of heart and mind which just rests and believes in Christ.

I have heard, since I have been in America, so many people preach and speak as if God gives a special dispensation of favour and success to those who believe in Him. I have heard so-called evangelists talk as if God provides the money out of the blue for journeying here and there, as if God makes special favours for them. They pull strings or commit outright cadging and then when it succeeds they say the Lord has sent this cheque or that. It is a kind of habit of human pride. If they could only hear a gramophone record of themselves, they would know how stupid they sound.

They should know that there are millions who are in poverty who are deeply Christian, totally surrendered, who are praying for God's help, but in this world we may not always see the result of our prayers.

That text is indeed true that "all things work together

for good to them that love God and are called according to His purpose." What works together for good in God's eyes is something very different from what works together for good in our eyes. You see, faith in Christ at times has got to be completely blind, completely trusting. If you go down into that text a little deeper and not just skim the surface—"All things work together for good to them that love God"—you may have to ask yourself, "Do I really love God enough for all things to work together for good?" "Am I called according to His purpose?" "Have I really fitted my life to the plan He has for me?"

I wonder how many of us could honestly answer that before the almighty person of God and say: "I love You with all my heart: I am called, I am living Your way, I therefore claim that all things shall work together for good for me." Do let us be careful that we do not have a kind of faith in Christ that is only for bright days.

I want you to have a faith that will hold so that you can still believe in Him when you are lying in a bed of pain or when you know that your cancer is going to be a long, slow, and painful business. Don't think it is easy—it is difficult. He understands if you cry out to Him at times, "Oh God, why are these pains gnawing at me?"

I write this, hoping that some day, someone may read it, when in like condition, and find help.

When you are tempted to let your suffering make you cry out against God or imagine that God should exempt His followers, remember, others more saintly than you have suffered terribly and won through. It is winning through that matters. You cannot win if you are a groaner against God. It is the easiest thing in the world to blame God for your suffering or even for allowing it. Surely you can do better than that.

So I come back to where I started. Do not imagine for one moment that being a Christian means that you have not got to face the problems that come to human beings in this world. It does mean that it gives you a greater power and strength to face these things—the knowledge that underneath are His everlasting arms to support you.

CHAPTER 7

Fellowship and Friends

THE chapter which has always been the greatest comfort to me is Philippians 2, verses 1-13, and in case you have not got your Bible handy let me give you the verses. I often ask my wife to read them to me as she says goodnight to me in this hospital, when I can hardly think, either from pain or barbiturates.

You will notice that the chapter starts by getting on good terms with you, in that it reminds us that there have been times of consolation, love, and fellowship in our walk with Christ and His followers. I am reminded of the times I sheltered in the knowledge of Christ amid the turmoil of the world, and I am sufficiently grateful to listen to what Paul now has to say to me. Memories come tumbling into my mind of the wonderful fellowship I have experienced with those of like mind, whose desire is to spread the influence of His kingdom in our day and generation.

How vital is this fellowship among Christians! It should be the sweetest, most harmonious company anywhere in the world, with the one uniting bond which rises above racial and class differences and national loyalties. This chapter is to me the yardstick for the relationship between Christian people, and the central focus of all is, of course, humility, death, and glorious triumphant resurrection of Jesus.

If there be therefore any consolation in Christ, if any comfort of love, if any fellowship of the Spirit, if any bowels and mercies,

Fulfil ye my joy, that ye be likeminded, having the same love, being of one accord, of one mind.

Let nothing be done through strife or vainglory; but in lowliness of mind let each esteem other better than themselves.

Look not every man on his own things, but every man also on the things of others.

Let this mind be in you, which was also in Christ Jesus:

Who, being in the form of God, thought it not robbery to be equal with God:

But made himself of no reputation, and took upon him the form of a servant, and was made in the likeness of men:

And being found in fashion as a man, he humbled himself, and became obedient unto death, even the death of the cross.

Wherefore God also hath highly exalted him, and given him a name which is above every name:

That at the name of Jesus every knee should bow, of things in heaven, and things in earth, and things under the earth;

And that every tongue should confess that Jesus Christ is Lord, to the glory of God the Father.

Wherefore, my beloved, as ye have always obeyed, not as in my presence only, but now much more in my absence, work out your own salvation with fear and trembling.

For it is God which worketh in you both to will and to do of his good pleasure.

PHILIPPIANS 2:1-13

Let us brood on that second verse:

Fulfil ye my joy, that ye be likeminded, having the same love, being of one accord, of one mind.

I would remind you, if I can, of the tremendous power there is of having fellowship with other Christians, with those who believe somewhat as you do.

If there is any comfort in the love of Christ, be like-

minded with others—don't stay outside the Church and be
a little person all to yourself, with no denomination: take
courage and join the fellowship of some church.

Naturally I turn to my church, the Church of England
and the Episcopal Church, and amongst Christians I find
friends that exceed all that the world has ever been able to
give me. I enjoy making friends, I love people.

Americans are the most friendly people in the world,
and it makes life more enjoyable. Among Christian people
within the Christian Church, there is a fellowship that ex-
ceeds the bonds of sight and hand. Christians find they
have an affinity with each other—so much in common that
they are friends right away.

At the time of my operation all my many friends prayed
for me and my wife. I know that she felt a strange assurance all the day of the operation, as she knelt in the
chapel of the Good Samaritan Hospital. It was the prayers
of those Christian friends that upheld her, that supported
her and gave her that firm assurance that in this case God
was going to bring her husband back to her. Was this
imagination? Is there not a case that can be made for corporate spiritual telepathy—to put prayer on the lowest
level?

Don't let yourself be without the fellowship of other
Christians. We should go very deep in our love for another
human being, we should go even deeper in our fellowship
with other Christians.

Of course, we are reserved with those who have let us
down—we hesitate to extend our trust twice. But we do put
our trust in Christ and we learn, through Him, to love His
people. Thus do I learn to love my fellow Christian people.
I thank God for the fellowship of Christian people in
Britain and America. The friends that you make in a moment of time as a minister of the Gospel are a great encouragement. It is a wonderful fellowship, and I hope and

pray that the fellowship between the churches in America and the churches in Britain will grow.

Naturally I find within my church those friends of Jesus who give each other so much of their love and their fellowship, and the fellowship extends beyond the bonds of just one church, to all those in other churches. I experienced this with the people of Marvin Methodist Church in Tyler, Texas—four wonderful days spent with them preaching, visiting, and looking down oil wells. Little did they know what was going on inside me at that time, but it was right they should not know, that it should be a time of happiness. God had a message for me to bring to them and they enjoyed it.

So it is that Christians meet together beyond the bounds of denomination, for if this mind be in you which was in Christ Jesus, we are all one. That chapter, Philippians 2, turns you to Christ Himself when it says: He thought it not robbery to be equal with God but became a servant, came in the likeness of man, and suffered as a man. I read that chapter over and over again, and thank God for all the depths of fellowship that it gives between us and Christ. Let us thank Christ for His example and for the fellowship that He gives us with Saints and Christians of our own and all other ages in our own and other countries. I hope that some lonely person who reads this may be drawn closer into the family of His Church and be found around our Lord's table, partaking of the one service that He alone instituted, so that in that mystical way they may become part of the Body of Christ. Through a devoted chaplain in the hospital, I was able to receive that Communion.

As members incorporate in the mystical body of Our Lord, we have a duty as well as a new relationship to each other. We stoop in humility to help one another over the difficult hurdles of life, as brother holding hands with brother. It is a costly thing to be a member of the Christian

Church, for we not only have obligations to God but to each other. Jesus was "big enough" to be a servant and so must we be lowly enough to serve one another and give out of our own storehouse to the needs of others. Jesus generously gave himself even to the death on the Cross. We dare not hold back our gifts to Christ's cause and to the needs of our fellow Christians. Is any sick among you? Then go and visit him and pray for him.

Loyalty to the company of Christ's Church on earth is one of the hallmarks of a true Christian. I find in America the most amazing loyalty to the churches among the members, and they see to it that the Church of Christ lacks nothing. In England the churches have existed for so long that they are almost expected to stand upright without this generation giving of their loyalty and substance to maintain them.

I should like to transplant for a period a vast number of American and British church people in each other's country and then hope for better things when each returned home.

Loyalty to the example of Christ means that we should foregather in company with His followers so that we may bow our knees together and reach out hands to help each other. We help one another not merely by our gifts to them but by showing ourselves friendly—giving friendship. Attention to friendships ought to be one of the distinguishing marks of a Christian.

I wonder if you have found yourself in hospital with few friends and been tempted to turn to self-pity or to cursing the shallowness of your acquaintances. Maybe the reason is that you have never really shown yourself friendly—pretending to yourself that you are shy and that it is for others to make the first move. Such a lot of self-deception!

We have to go out to meet people from the heart and remember that the basis of friendship is loyalty. It is a wonderful thing to have one person in the world who knows the worst about you and will stick up for you. Of course, fundamentally there is only one person like that, and He is Christ. But by God's grace, we can find a great degree of this loyalty, this friendship amongst our frail, fellow human beings. You are more likely to find this deep friendship amongst Christians than amongst the godless. The people who say you do not have to go to church to be a Christian give themselves away. Obviously they do not know Christ well enough themselves or they would have this desire to link up with His friends. If they ever go to heaven they are going to feel awfully out of step with many who are there.

The Red Indians in Arizona incidentally hold hands; they do not shake the fellowship away—and this I liked . . . it communicates trust and friendship.

Try not to indulge in self-pity if you feel all alone in the world with your trouble. He is there in some weird and wonderful way if you seek Him, and if He raises up to you at this moment some new-found friend in a nurse, in a visitor—guard that friend, love that friend, and hold on. And perhaps for the first time in your life, give back in loyalty and affection. Do not excuse yourself from giving by saying you do not want to get hurt. What does it matter if you gain a friend and enjoy living on the deeps, even if it does not last for ever?

It is tragic that there is so much lack of affection in millions of homes, even amongst husbands and wives and their children. In the community of followers of Jesus there is a depth of understanding and fellowship when the Master is in control and all are agreed with Him. Can two "walk together" except they be agreed?

Yet it is better to be utterly alone in the world than to have sham friends and no sympathy, for in coming to the end of ourselves, we come to the beginning of God.

To me friendship means loyalty, and I feel that it is expected of me not to run my friends down behind their backs. In fact I should stick up for them, look after their interests, and go out of my way to help them. I would like to feel this towards those who call me by my Christian name, but unfortunately this is not a yardstick in certain circles, for some people use Christian names in two minutes without it being any indication of a basis of friendship.

Let us see to it that we go out of our way to give in friendship to another cancer patient so as to widen the scope of our present friendships.

There must be many cancer sufferers who would give the world to have as a friend a really convinced loyal Christian who had been through the hoop of cancer and won through. They would have so much in common and could help each other over so many stiles. There is something uplifting in being able to give as well as receive friendship.

It was Dr. Johnson who said that friendship was such a valuable yet delicate a thing that it was in need of constant repair.

I think it is impossible to overestimate the importance of friends in life. It is really quite extraordinary how two people can suddenly hit it off with each other and the spontaneous interaction of their personalities brings a new sparkle to their spirit. Men are more capable of deep friendship for each other than women. But no matter if the sexes are mixed, it is the "sparkle" reaction which is important. It is stimulating. It breeds respect and affection and sends you on your way bubbling inside.

So let us write to our friends more letters, make more phone calls, and arrange more meetings.

CHAPTER 8

Time to Wear the Prodigal's Shoes

Two weeks before I went into hospital I preached at All Saints', Beverly Hills, on the story of the prodigal's shoes, and little did I realise that this sermon might have a greater meaning for me within two weeks.

Bring forth the best robe and put it on him; and put a ring on his hand and shoes on his feet.

What I want you to think about is the prodigal's shoes. Shoes often show something of the character of those who wear them, and these particular shoes in this story are very important.

I have in my bottom drawer a tiny shoe which belonged to my little boy when he was about one. He grew out of it and I have kept it and hoped to have it pickled one day in silver, as a kind of ash tray. I wonder if you have a similar shoe. As you look at it, you remember how he put his legs out a little bit and so today you can see that outer edge which has been worn down. It shows the character of the little child, and you have preserved this memory. Sometimes we wish we had preserved a great many more things in our lives.

But to return to the prodigal's shoes. May I remind you of the story? The man was bored with home, for he was young, growing up, and feeling that the world was going by and he was missing it in his remote place on his father's farm. Dissatisfied, restless, he made that one mistake that so many make, thinking that what would satisfy him was far away and over the hills. So, without thought of asking his father's advice, what his father's will was, what he had planned for his patrimony, he demanded of his father every penny that he needed for the journey. He got the money by saying "Give me," and he went away. When he had received what was due to him and had spent it, he began to be in want and he remembered his father. He went through that experience which most people go through before they reach God: that coming to the end of himself he came to the beginning of God.

This is the story that Jesus told us as the picture of the home and heart of God. Before, all the prodigal wanted was his own will in the home, the only evidence of love that he wanted was to be given what he asked for. Was he a spoilt boy? We do not know the background history, but we have seen history repeated again and again. He learned through the hard school of life that now he was ignorant. He goes back to the father and says, "Make me." He changes his request from "Give me" to "Make me." "You are right, I was all wrong, I was all mixed up. I want to be your servant. I do not expect to be made a son again." But the glorious thing about this story was that he was made the son again. He was not made a servant. He would have been content to become a hired servant, but his father re-created him as a son. What were the signs of his sonship? They were the robe on his back, the ring on his finger, and the shoes on his feet.

This is the welcome that each one of us can expect from God. Don't be a Thomas, a Doubting Thomas. Don't be a chap who hides behind, "I am not good enough to ask God's forgiveness." You do not have to wait until you are good. God has such a welcome for you—not as a servant. He will make you into a son, so that you know in whom you have to believe, and you will be strong in that belief, for He will give you the evidences. He will give you a new robe on your back, a new ring on your finger, and shoes on your feet.

Now these shoes are very important. They are important because they mean something to the Christian. As a new-born, forgiven Christian, you will want to come into church, to take the Communion; this mystical ceremony and service which He alone instituted. It is the one service that exists throughout the world. This is the only service that He ever created. To be given the prodigal's shoes does not mean that you have only got to go to church.

The shoes are for wearing. My little boy grew out of his shoes. The prodigal wore his original shoes out and he did not have any more, and the father gave him a new pair. God gives us a new pair of shoes in which to travel back to the far country.

I want you to think for a moment in imagination of the other side of the prodigal's story.

You know the story backwards. You feel sorry for the elder brother, you go through all the emotions that we all go through as we hear the story. But will you pause for a moment and think of the father. He provided the old shoes and now they were worn out, so he provided the new shoes. In true scriptural manner, he rejoiced because he had found the coin which he had lost—he had lost his son and now he rejoiced because he had found him again, so there was music and dancing.

There was happiness, and I am glad that Christ told this story, but there was not happiness everywhere. The older brother was angry. Let us imagine that the father went out and bumped into another father who said, "That's all very well. Your child has come back: but your boy took mine with him and my son has not come back. What are you going to do about it?"

Let us assume that the father himself went to that far country because he was intrigued to know the kind of life his son had lived. Let us imagine what happened there, and go with the father over the hills. He found an inn and he registered and when he put his name down, immediately the innkeeper drew himself up in a pursed kind of way. He had recognised the name and the father experienced the wretchedness of being ashamed of his son. The fellow had left debts at the inn and an unsavoury reputation everywhere.

There was no doubt about this in the father's mind, there was no doubt about the reaction of the innkeeper. So the father said: "How much did he owe?" and he paid the debt, bitterly aware in his heart that money could not pay for the damage done in the far country. He went down the street, paused by a local shop. By that time the news in this little village had got round and he was ostracised. He passed through the shop and set things right as far as he could in terms of money, and then he sat down in a café. There he found a coarse young fellow whom he hardly dared to recognise. He knew it was his friend's son whom his own son had led into utter degradation. His language, his manner, and his whole radiation was such that it made him shrivel inside. "There, but for the grace of God, is my son, and there still is my friend's son," he thought to himself. He tried to reason with the boy, but would this fellow listen? No. This was a debt which could not be settled with money, for he was dealing with a human personality. Dispirited and tired of the trail that his son had left behind, he went out of the village and sat on the well. Then a woman came along with a child on her back. She was sad, she knew who he was but she was too pent up to talk. He did not have to ask whose the child was on her back and, sick at heart, he went home.

If what I have imagined about the far country ever took place, I am sure he would remind his boy of the responsibility of wearing the new shoes on his feet. He was shod now with the preparation of the Gospel, and the Gospel is good news for the godless. Let us hope that he sends his son back into the far country to the human kind, to do what the father could not do with money—to tell of the way of Christ, the way of God in that far country.

Those shoes are to be worn. Can we ever wear them long enough? People who have been in the far country and those who have been pretty good all their lives, need to come to God to ask Him for forgiveness so that they may receive the shoes.

It so happens that the other day I received a letter which had been sent on to me from England. Now this woman writes to me out of the blue after twenty-one years, and I hardly remember the signature. She luckily had time to wear the shoes, as you will see:

Dear Mr Hession,

First I had better explain that I used to be a member of your St Margaret's Church in London. I thought I would write to you as it will be twenty-one years ago on the 26th July that God used you to help me. I very nearly did not come into that meeting that night. I shall never forget walking up and down Lee High Road trying to decide whether to go or not. I was on the point of giving up my Sunday School class, the Church and everything connected with it, and it did not really seem worth while to go to the meeting either. Finally I decided to go, just this once, and make it the last.

How different were my feelings when the meeting was over, and I have proved that He is indeed 'sweeter as the years go by' as we used to sing at St Margaret's.

I am now married and I have two boys, one twelve and the

other eight-and-a-half, and we also have a little foster child, a boy of nine-and-a-half. My husband is a teacher and has been transferred to this new senior school near Plymouth. He teaches religious knowledge throughout the school and he has three hundred children from eleven to fifteen. What a wonderful opportunity and he hopes to use Dawn Trust film strips. He is allocated money each year with which to buy them. He is a lay reader and as there are many vicars in this part with two churches and no curate, he is in great demand every Sunday. . . .

And so she goes on. Now there was somebody to whom God granted at least twenty-one years to use the shoes that God gives to the man or woman who asks for forgiveness. That meeting was a turning point in her life.

Here is another case. In my parish in Aylesbury during the war, they built an enormous hospital with eleven hundred beds, almost overnight, under the emergency scheme, and I had to be chaplain of it, without any curate and with a twenty-thousand-population parish. I took Communion round the wards there at six o'clock in the morning, and one incident stands out in my mind above almost all others.

After the British and Canadian raid on Dieppe on the coast of France, we had hundreds of soldiers and sailors burnt all over because the Germans were tipped off about the raid and were ready for our men and put burning oil on the water. As I went into one ward, the sister said, "Oh, Padre, the third bed on the right wants to talk to you."

As I sat on his bed, its occupant said: "Do you remember me, Padre?" I fumbled in my mind to remember. There were in this case only two eyes to recognise and the burnt man was lying in a bed of cellophane so that the air should not reach his burns. "Do you remember one day in London?"—and then he reminded me, and this was the story.

From time to time we used to go up to London from Aylesbury to show a film service in some of the air-raid shelters in the middle of the blitz. We showed an old-fashioned life of Jesus film called *From Manger to Cross*. I had stretched the film to run at talkie speed and put a running biblical commentary on the sound track.

The people loved to watch that film and they would forget the noise of the bombs and the shaking of the ground as they watched it. One evening before the end, there slipped out a couple who had been there for two or three nights running, and as they passed me they said, "Cheerio." When you are working a projector, you are rather busy and there is not much time to talk till the show is finished. I had seen them before. They picked their way in the blackout, two young things very much in love, and at last, after stepping over broken glass and rubble, they got to Victoria Station. His leave had finished, both were in uniform and the parting moment was coming for them. The station had no glass left in the roof, but they managed to find their way in the darkness and by the bookstall they paused for a last kiss.

Neither knew whether they would see the other again, but both wished that they had got married during their four days' leave. Now the parting came. She stayed at the barrier. They wanted to say so many things to each other and all he remembered was her trim little figure waving "Goodbye" while she forced back the tears and he caught his train.

The man was posted to Egypt. Now Egypt was hot, the desert war was not pleasant, and boring at times, especially at the beginning of the campaign as the army fought back and forth about Bengasi. Bored, tired, away from home, away from the restrictions of his friends, this soldier found himself in Cairo during his leave periods. What could he do? There was a woman on the corner, he knew what she was and what she wanted, but he picked her up and together they got drunk. The next morning he felt pretty sick about it all, but he told himself that everyone else did it and there was a war on. So he went on downhill in his far country. He was morose, fed up with himself, and when he wrote to his girl, he tried to pretend he was just the same. Then, finally, he was wounded and invalided home.

He arranged to meet his girl, and then came the disappointment: the girl found he had changed and they did not hit it off. He was different. There was something that had become coarse inside him. He took a train up to Cheshire to see his parents in their humble little home. It seemed disappointing and rather squalid after the places he had seen and he did not seem to get on well with his mother any longer.

He was in a mess. He had quarrelled with his girl, quarrelled with his mother, and he was no good to anybody.

He came back to London, fed up, and then he heard that there was a call for volunteers for the "tip-and-run" raids on the coast of France. So he volunteered, thinking that there was nothing left but to die. He had wanted to come home so badly, but when he came home he found that home did not exist for him any more.

Now anybody who has been through this experience will know what the prodigal felt. And then he was thrown into the sea and burnt, and he kept pleading to me: "Will God ever forgive me?" I was able, with God's help, to tell that fellow how he could unload to Christ to claim his forgiveness so that he would receive the robe on his back, the ring of his forgiveness, and the shoes on his feet. Of course, one day he hoped to go back to his many friends, showing the ring, wearing the shoes, but unfortunately he did not have time to wear the shoes. He died a few days later.

The woman who wrote that letter to me after twenty-one years was lucky. So far she has had twenty-one years to wear the shoes. This poor soldier prodigal had no time in which to make amends for the past.

How long have you and I got to wear the shoes that God provides for those who become Christians? Let us pray that He will grant to us time in this life, which so badly needs a sincere loyal Christian, to wear the shoes and work for Him, to work for His Church. You and I must live very close to Him and ask His forgiveness, claim those shoes, and make good use of them. When I get out of this hospital I am determined to live a long time and wear the new shoes of an extended life which He has given me for some hidden purpose. My far country will be to help those who suffer, especially because of cancer, and if it be possible, to bring them a living faith and a new hope.

CHAPTER 9

Going the Extra Mile

ONCE again the hospital is bedded down and that eerie stillness so familiar to hospitals anywhere in the world has settled in for another night. The night sister has done her rounds and the visual eye of the recorder glows on my bedside locker as I think aloud about "going the extra mile"—for this spirit is the epitome of being a Christian. I really should be asleep, but the drugs do not work and the idea of talking to you through this book has become all-important to me. I look forward to this nightly session with my unseen reader. I play back the recording of the night before and try to visualise my reader of the future.

I have been brooding over that wonderful chapter which Paul wrote in his first letter to the Christian believers of Corinth. It is the thirteenth chapter, and you may know it by heart from childhood. In case you have forgotten it, here it is. I have used the modern word "love" instead of the old-fashioned word "charity" which is used in the Authorised Version. Charity today is only part of love in our vocabulary, whereas in the old days it covered the whole of love.

First let us read it as if it were only talking about love between two people—husband and wife—the love we bear to our partner. All sorts of amazing implications, understandings, and lessons will be apparent for our married life.

Married love has to bear such a lot of things—trust for so many things, hope for the best—put up with a great deal. True love really should never fail. It is a high pedestal for love.

Though I speak with the tongues of men and of angels and have not love, I am become as sounding brass or a tinkling cymbal.

And though I have the gift of prophecy and understand all mysteries and all knowledge: and though I have all faith, so that I could remove mountains, and have not love, I am nothing.

And though I bestow all my goods to feed the poor, and though I give my body to be burned, and have not love, it profiteth me nothing.

Love suffereth long, and is kind; love envieth not; love vaunteth not itself, is not puffed up,

Doth not behave itself unseemly, seeketh not her own, is not easily provoked, thinketh no evil;

Rejoiceth not in iniquity, but rejoiceth in the truth;

Beareth all things, believeth all things, hopeth all things, endureth all things.

Love never faileth: but whether there be prophecies, they shall fail; whether there be tongues, they shall cease; whether there be knowledge, it shall vanish away.

For we know in part, and we prophesy in part.

But when that which is perfect is come, then that which is in part shall be done away.

When I was a child, I spake as a child, I understood as a child, I thought as a child; but when I became a man, I put away childish things.

For now we see through a glass darkly; but then face to face; now I know in part; but then shall I know even as also I am known.

And now abideth faith, hope, love, these three; but the greatest of these is love.

I CORINTHIANS 13

Please read it again and realise it is talking about something far bigger, the very quality of life for the Christian when the spirit of Christ or of God—love—bubbles up in his heart. When you and I are spiritually born again, we must let this love-flow stream upwards in us.

Love beareth all things. It means that you and I, as we live in life, should bear sufferings, should bear rudeness by other people.

When it says, "Love hopeth all things," it means that you and I must count on and expect the very best, we must be optimistic. You "can't be optimistic if you've got a misty optic." If your spiritual eye is clouded, you cannot be optimistic in the spiritual sense. Nothing clouds out God more than impurity of mind, talk, or action. It is living death to Christian spiritual life. So many people expect the worst in life not merely from the weather but from others, and they are so depressing to be with, for every life increases the momentum of good or ill in the world. No sin or suffering ever leaves us where it finds us, so don't let it blunt the edge of your vision and warp your personality. Rise above it.

So, in reading this chapter through again and again, let us interpret it as Christ's message for those who would live with the bubbling out of the love of God in their lives. Let those of us who are married read it together and ask for strength to live by its precepts.

May I add to it this little poem which I have written in my Bible many, many years ago:

> Love ever Gives
> > Forgives
> > Outlives
> > Ever stands
> > With open hands
> > And while it lives
> > It gives

For this is love's prerogative
To give
And give
And give.

This is true of married life, for the kind of love you should bear your partner is such that it stands, with open hands . . . is such that it outlives any quarrels and differences which grown-up personalities living under the same roof must undoubtedly have with each other. For one of the greatest problems of the world is for human personalities living under the same roof to get on with each other at all times in perfect harmony. It is an art to be learned and practised till our dying day. It stands for married love, when you have to forgive each other far beyond little things. When you each have to outlive: it does not mean that you just have to stand there and forgive the other person, but outlive.

You have to be big enough to let "it" ride out of your life and so outlive that thing so that it is never remembered again. Some passing infatuation, some jealous rage, some quick retort, some stupid forgetfulness. Outlive it. Don't make mountains out of molehills. Look for the best in the one that has caused the rift between you and pour the oil of Christian forgiveness quickly into the wound before it festers.

How often I have seen pride drive a wedge between two people when neither will climb down and say: "Sorry, darling, I got in a bate—I didn't mean it." Pride is such a stupid thing for lovers. It wastes so much time and causes so much hurt to both. "Let not the sun go down on your wrath" should be rewritten for married people: "Let not the light go out and sleep come till you have bridged any gulf between you." The touch of a foot, the squeeze of a hand, and a mumbled apology can so often save the next day.

You do not need a marriage-guidance clinic with a lot of theoretical spinsters or bachelor priests. A healthy pair of scissors used freely on your pride, blind jealousy, biting tongue, or bad temper will work wonders, especially if you both have a steady sense of humour.

Once two people have set up home and life together, everyone and everything outside that circle does not matter —these two stand or fall together, they are bound up with each other. Loyalty to one another is absolutely paramount. You will do things for each other far beyond what could ever be expected and you will love doing it. The extra mile of love is not wearisome, it is like freewheeling downhill on a bicycle with the wind in your hair. Self-sacrifice for love's sake brings a sense of gaiety and releases the springs of happiness.

I want you to think again about that line, "Having the same love, being of one accord, of one mind." It is awfully difficult sometimes to remain in love, because human frailty enters in. Just because we have fallen in love, it does not say that we do not take with us that same grisly spirit that we had as a boy, that same selfish spirit we had as a girl. Just because we have fallen in love, it does not make us different people—and that is the tragedy. Sometimes we do not realise that love has to overcome and deepen as the days go by, and for that we need God. Love is such an unselfish thing.

Love ever gives, and if you were to ask your pastor: "Should I forgive this, should I forgive that?" the only possible answer is that "Love ever gives, forgives, outlives, ever stands with open hands" to that loved one to take them once again within your grasp. There is nothing too much for God to forgive us.

Should not we forgive others their trespasses against us? We are supposed to pray that Lord's Prayer and mean it, and if once we shut love out of our life, because of some failure in another, it is very difficult to get it back, because love gives itself and if not given, "No genius, beauty, state or wit, no gold of earth or gem of Heaven is rich enough to purchase it."

So do let us be careful in the quarrels in our home, in the little spurts of irritability which so often ruffle the surface of life and then cause such far-reaching results. Let us be careful to nurse this truth, because, when we look around the world, it is full of such disagreeable things.

When you come down to it, what is really worth while in your life is not necessarily your home, the furniture, the sticks, but the love that someone bears for you and you bear for him.

Guard that as you would your life. It is more valuable than your life, and Christ can help you in this: let this mind be in you which was also in Christ Jesus, for though He was God He thought it no robbery to be equal with God but became His servant and dwelt among us. A wonderful example of humility and of ordinary life, working out in this world.

No, you cannot buy love with presents, but only with your very self—and *then* presents have a part. In much the same way, you cannot buy the saving power of God's love into your life by a series of good works. You have to give up your very being to God, and then His spirit and love flows out through you and good works automatically follow. We often know when a person is "putting it on" or really does things from the heart—sincerity has a ring all of its own.

What goes for married love also goes in a much bigger way for living out the Christian way of life. Christianity not only appeals to those who are married, but to the unmarried, those to whom the gift of love has never come.

They can find in Him the sublimation of all they need and want in life by going out in service to their fellow men to give, and give, and give, even though there is no reward in this life. One's fellow men are as often as not ungrateful, so do not be disheartened if they do not clap you on the back.

Mark you, there is no reward as far as we can see, that Christ stores up for people in this world, but whether you like the idea or not, He has got a reward in Heaven although you and I do not do things for that reward in Heaven. That is not our incentive. Yet our Master once said: "Great is your reward in Heaven," so it would appear that in the world to come there are compensations for some of the things of this world.

So if, when you are down, you wonder whether going the extra mile for somebody else is worth while, just remind yourself that this life is not the only life, that there is another world.

In what way can you go the extra mile? By doing things from the heart.

There is the old story of a little child staggering along the road carrying a smaller child in its arms, the passer-by saying: "You've got a heavy load, haven't you?" and the child replying: "That's not a load, it's my brother." For like reasons when you and I go the extra mile, it is not all that tough, for we are motivated by love. The hallmarks of going the extra mile are generosity, hospitality, and sympathy.

What an attractive sight a generous child is when sweets and toys are shared with its fellows to a point where the child has none for itself. It hardly notices this lack for the unself-conscious pleasure of giving to others.

Greediness and meanness are such revolting, ugly characteristics! I hate to think of a person being short of money, especially a child with its pocket money. When I find my eleven-year-old daughter is short of money, I feel a pain inside me. "It's quite all right, Daddy, I don't want to buy anything." Every now and again I find receipts arriving for her from a cat-protection league, for it is there she sends any spare cash, and not to her post-office book.

When I find myself wishing she would save it when I have little to give, I remind myself it is better for her growing character to be this way.

"The Lord loves a cheerful giver," and He valued the widow's mite in the temple. If you want to go the extra mile, give generously "till it darned well hurts."

Once you begin to be generous in gifts you will find it unleashes hidden springs of character. No need for a facial massage. You will never want for friends, for it will lead to your being generous of praise and sympathy. You will become a hospitable person not merely in welcoming people into your home but into the warmth of your personality. You will be a contributor to life and never contemptuous of your fellows.

Today we have trade unions: I am a member of the Cinematograph Technicians' Union, with a cameraman's and director's ticket. I have to be a member today to work in any studio. I hope that through my membership I may, without entering into their politics, help somehow to keep their conditions right.

How often some trade unions have insisted on just a minumum amount of time and work for the maximum amount of pay. This spirit is the curse which threatens our Western free world. There are so many people who only do just so much work in so many hours for just so much money, and it is said they are few and far between who will go the extra mile, who will see that a job is well done, who will stay after working hours to see the job done, without expecting overtime pay, but just for the integrity of their personality. It is those few who are the salt of the earth, not the politicians, not the shop stewards. They are the salt of the earth, and if you want to be a sincere person, if you want to increase the momentum for good in this world, then go the extra mile.

Be the kind of nurse who has kindly hands and does a thoroughly good job of real work, the doctor who reaches out beyond what is just required of him, the worker who does more than a day's work for a day's wages, who does little extra things out of personal integrity.

Some people's standard of plain ordinary work is chronic. The Christian should be one who builds the reputation of CHRISTIAN, not only by doing a first-class job in whatever occupation he is in, but also by adding those extra things which show the mainspring of his motives. The world in every department is utterly starved of such people—to find such a person in a carpenter, secretary, cook, etc., is like finding a precious stone. Do not expect others to fall over themselves to thank you but do not let that put you off. Personal integrity before your maker is what counts.

It may not pay in this world, and God preserve us from having our hands outstretched for tips for the extra mile. Let's go that extra mile because there bubbles up in our hearts a love for Christ, which means that we want to witness for Him, not by saying, "I am a Christian, I am converted," but by being a different kind of person. The Church of Christ needs identified Christians as witnesses —and by identified Christians I mean those who are not ashamed to own up to this allegiance to Christ and to one of His visible churches on earth, but also prepared to prove it by this different quality of life.

So I come to the end of my stay in hospital—they have been more than kind and I almost hate to go. I will miss my doctor and all the friends in America, but I will come back. I want to see Florida, Yellowstone, Honolulu, and renew so many friendships. What a pity there are six thousand miles or so between Hollywood and England. But I shall pray and save for our return, and hope to have the strength to fulfil many lecture and preaching engagements.

Like so many patients, I will be like a ship without an anchor when I lose my nurse, who has given so much more than the extra mile. My pains and my wife's anxieties were hers, and no man could have been ill in a more friendly, comfortable, and efficient hospital.

How can I show my gratitude? I must find a way to go the extra mile to help other cancer patients and so live my gratitude. From the moment I was allowed to get out of bed, I walked and walked the corridors in the dressing gown given me by John Payne, so that I could build my muscles enough to withstand the long plane journey to London. Many a time I fell asleep over the tape recorder and the night sister came in and found it running and switched it off. I think that the most enjoyable moment in the hospital was the time when I was allowed my first bath, sitting on an air ring and singing at the top of my voice. Americans do not understand the word bath—they call it a tub. Their standard of hospitalisation, medication, and nursing is really terrific, and there is none of that rigid discipline where neither patients nor nurses dare ask for an extra thing.

The Americans certainly have a very high standard of medical services. I hope that I have shown them that a Britisher can get well dead on schedule and become self-supporting in physical matters. I leave this hospital, for a few days' rest at a friend's house, with a very grateful heart.

CHAPTER 10

From Britain

THE four weeks and five days in hospital passed with the usual ups and downs of a relapse, crisis, and steady walking of the corridors in a determination to get away on schedule by plane five weeks after the operation.

"You're not leaving America for good? Don't you like us then? Don't you like our country, or perhaps you're just going back to collect your things," said a senior nurse. I fumbled for the right words of explanation as I had often done to the same question from the man at the drugstore on Sunset Boulevard, from the electricians at the studio. It was obviously inconceivable to them that anyone, rich or poor, could possibly want to live elsewhere than in California or anywhere than in America for that matter.

I explained that there was no place like your own home and that I loved Britain, even if the people were not so warmhearted and the climate a bit depressing and the roads a trifle narrow. But I would come back, I said, as soon as I was well and as soon as I had my new projects running properly.

There had been talk of my running a series of missions in Episcopal churches in eighteen months' time, but that was before I went into hospital. I had been asked to "crew" on a lawyer friend's yacht in the 1955 Race to Tahiti and back. . . .

The lights of the Los Angeles airport were beginning to twinkle as my surgeon—armed with special drugs and an orchid for my wife—my nurse, and a group of friends bade us farewell. I walked on the plane and retired to my cabin and my surgeon made sure I was safely tucked in. The plane's engines vibrated my memories into a muddled kaleidoscope of fabulous scenery enjoyed, of a host of wonderfully enthusiastic friends, mixed with remembered snatches of conversation:

. . . the warm hand of a kindly bishop sitting by my bed who admitted he was of British stock and knew what I felt about Anglo-American relations, especially amongst church people.

. . . the Negro church in Washington where the congregation would not let me preach till I had taught them how to sing, unaccompanied, a chorus, "How greatly Jesus must have loved me—to bear my sins." We had to sing it over and over again. After the service I showed them my colour films of the Coronation. At the end they were so enthusiastic they sang and clapped about the crown which Jesus was going to put on their heads when they got to Glory! What fun! Happy, simple people, who, like every church in America, took a visiting British preacher to their hearts.

. . . the pet porcupine which crawled round the dining hall of that little inn far away in the wilds of the Rockies.

. . . the sheriff in Nebraska who apologised for fining me fourteen dollars for cruising at 90 m.p.h. at the end of a day when we had already covered 656 miles since leaving Chicago.

. . . the monocle of the British Consul after church in Beverly Hills, which would not stay in his eye as he kept saying, "Good show, good sermon, me boy."

. . . the Chief Justice of America at a garden party in Washington, who seemed as delighted as one's own father that we were going to his beloved California.

. . . the delightful but crazy man we met in a log cabin in the mountains near Las Vegas, Nevada, who thought he was a second Christ destined to make a film of himself as Christ, complete with his beard. With the money he hoped to make he was going to buy the gambling hotels along the Las Vegas strip and then give the money they made in future years in grants to the Christian churches of the world.

. . . the bear which knocked over our dustbins during each evening that we stayed in a log cabin among the vast redwood trees in Sequoia which is north of Hollywood and the Mojave Desert towards Yosemite and San Francisco. Here chipmunks ran into the cabin wanting food, and wild deer hung around the open-air kitchens which were part of each log cabin.

. . . the open-air singsongs and barn dances in the Rocky Mountain camp where the organiser thought my wife was my daughter.

. . . the yacht racing in the Pacific off Santa Barbara, when we forgot our sandwiches and had to watch the rest of the crew eating theirs. But we made up for it when we got back to the palm-tree clubhouse for the food and prize giving. Our skipper got a prize, but we got our food.

. . . the log-cabin motel in the Rio Grande with its attractive suite where we stayed and tracked down marmots and mountain cats with our cameras.

. . . kneeling at midnight in the ornate Greek church to try and get our souls clean and our minds refreshed after attending a small private showing of *The Gladiators*, which Spyros Skouras had invited us to in the Fox Studios that evening just before its public release. This superb Greek church had been given by Spyros at the time of his tragic loss of his daughter.

. . . the bedroom where I spent the three days before being transported to the airport. The room with its view overlooking the whole of Hollywood below had been given up to me by Mary and Vincent Palmer, who had so kindly looked after Catrin while I was in hospital.

So many, many memories, which will live with us for ever and make us long to return to America. It is nearly twenty years since I first started going to America.

It is a country where friendship and a zest for life sweeps you off your feet. Yes—a zest for life—that is what one must have whatever one's restrictions or sufferings. Make every day worth while before God for one's family and for oneself, while one has the strength to live it.

At New York airport after the nonstop night flight from Los Angeles, an ambulance took me to a pre-arranged nursing home for a supposed eight-hour rest, but by some mistake it turned out to be a very downtown old folks' stopping place before the undertaker collected them. After a phone call, BOAC moved us to a hotel for what remained of the eight hours.

After the rest in New York we again set off at dusk in a gorgeous BOAC Monarch Stratocruiser. We slept well, in our bunk, and never shall we forget waking up and looking out of our berth window over the Atlantic with its brilliant early-morning sun. I turned to Catrin and said: "Just look at those cotton-wool clouds and the golden tints as the sun comes up. Isn't it fun to be alive?" We tucked down between the sheets and enjoyed the superb sunrise over the Atlantic. The noise of the plane was a quiet purr compared with the racket of the American plane from Los Angeles.

My mother-in-law, who is a doctor, met us with an ambulance at London Airport, and her face betrayed dismay as she saw me "walk" off the plane.

"For goodness sake, don't look so well," she said. "I had an awful job to get an ambulance and a hospital bed with this National Health scheme. You have to be nearly dying for that."

The American doctor had arranged with Sir Horace Evans that I should be medically checked in Britain, but twenty-four hours in hospital were enough check-up for me and I went down to my seaside home at Studland to convalesce and to work. The hospital in London was a bit of a contrast with its hard bed and ward full of old men—one of whom yelled all night for a bottle or something. He was, of course, senile and in a kind of cage, but it meant we got no sleep all night.

To those of you who may wonder what it is going to be like when you leave hospital and live with few internal organs and artificial pipes, I would say this:

It is not easy—I am not going to pretend it is. But life is worth living, worth fighting for if you fill every minute with something worth doing for God, for your wife, for your children, and for your work. I have been so busy that I have had little time to look inside except at times when one is confined to bed.

The secret, I feel, is never to look down, for the ice is jolly thin, in fact too thin to pause on. It reminds me of that saying of Paul: "Looking unto Jesus the author and finisher of our faith." He meant that in Christ we have a point on the horizon to concentrate upon—rather like sailing a boat and keeping your eye on a headland and making allowances for the wind and tide. Only Christ can give you the power to keep on making those allowances for the wind and tide. Only Christ can give you the power to keep on making those allowances when the tide is too strong. He did promise us that His strength is made perfect in our weakness.

So, when I am weak, depressed, or in pain, I cry out to God who alone understands. I wait on God for a daily renewal of courage.

Paul talks about running the race that is set before us—none of us knows how long that race is. We have got to be mentally and spiritually adjusted to life as it is and not live as an invalid unless it is absolutely necessary.

A colostomy can be lived with, although at times it is painful. The muscles can be trained. But it all needs a constant patience, discipline, and a mental adjustment to life. I can assure you it is better than dying and having to say goodbye to your wife, children, and friends.

This, I think, is the heart of suffering. We can find courage to bear the physical pain—but to know that you may any moment have to say goodbye to those who mean more to you than life itself is agony for you and for them. The agony of Jesus in the Garden of Gethsemane was this kind of agony—as God incarnate in human form, He had grown extremely fond of these rough country folk and was disturbed at the prospect of leaving them. Disturbed that they, through the frailty of human nature, were going to betray Him. This handful whom He particularly loved were going to be a disappointment to themselves and to Him—so much so that He was to bring into the world a new order. The order was the sending of the Holy Spirit to enter men's lives and invigorate them as a new dynamic power.

Poor failing weak humanity! Such aspirations for the highest, but such weakness in execution of those lofty ambitions. He groaned in spirit over the frailty of His friends. He prayed to His Father in heaven for them and for all of us who believe on Him through their word. Do read His prayers in St. John's Gospel and find the refreshment of Jesus praying for you and me.

He groaned in spirit—sweated great drops of blood—over the sins and frailty of the whole of humanity, for He knew that on the Cross in the mystery of heaven He was to bear the sins of the whole world. The load and the penalty of human sin would shut out the light of His Father's presence like a cloud as He hung on the Cross. But He would break through that cloud with these words of that psalm on His lips: "It is finished. Into Thy hands I commend My spirit."

I think that man's disloyalty and sin was at the heart of His agony. Here is a lesson lest we should put our human friends or life partners on pedestals. "The spirit indeed is willing, but the flesh is weak." Wonderful compassion. Even Christ in the hour of His spiritual suffering needed human hearts to be near Him—to watch and to pray. How much more do we need human companionship. He chose out three disciples to be near Him, but they fell asleep. It is not easy for some to bear suffering, because they have to bear it alone.

I was so very lucky—I had my wife with me all the time, and she never faltered. It was wonderful to greet my two children and to have their company; it made me realise more than ever how lucky I was to be alive.

To those who wonder how soon it takes after such an operation to get back into life, let me say five or six weeks. By that time I was forcing myself to walk over the moors by my cottage one, then two and three miles each day. To sit down with any degree of comfort took a bit longer.

I was told to rest completely—to convalesce for a year—but I could not do that. I had to get back into the stream of life and occupy every day to the full, just in case my new lease of life should run out.

I started preaching again at Christmas in St. Michael's, Bournemouth, and then in Exeter Cathedral.

Six months after my operation I was invited to St. Moritz and jumped at the opportunity, for there I could ski again. Brabazon and the Cresta Committee refused to let me go down the run because it was too dangerous, but I was able to ski down the many runs and to skate without tearing anything inside. I was scared stiff at times, especially skiing down the fast runs when it was snowing, but that is half the fun. I wanted to prove to myself that I really was alive—why, I do not quite know! It was a crazy thing to do, but luckily I had a good period then, and I returned to the hard work at home with more determination.

Wherever you are as you read this book, there is an absorbing work for Christ's kingdom going on close at hand. You can find a relief out of your suffering or problems by seeking it out, helping and identifying yourself with it. There is always a work for Jesus that you can do, whether it be with your hands, your money, or your prayers. To disobey the promptings of God in your heart is to harden your heart.

Start by doing someone a good turn and soon the habit will develop till you become a changed personality.

How you take suffering is awfully important, for it can make you a nicer, warmer, and more helpful personality. If you take it badly, you will radiate a disgruntled, embittered spirit which will only increase the suffering of the world. Trouble will sweeten or embitter you, and sufferings should be steppingstones to fresh endeavour, not stumbling blocks.

You can make it harder for others to bear bravely their burdens, for behind the scenes of many lives are burdens almost too heavy to be borne. Talk to yourself like a Dutch uncle and see if there is not some ground in your life upon which to stand and work with your hand upstretched to God. The soul or the heart can heal if you rest back on the very love of God for you. His companionship in a life torn by domestic unhappiness or suffering is absolutely vital.

I know from bitter experience that domestic unhappiness can blight and sour people's lives almost more than suffering, but the Christian has to have his own troubles so well in order that there is room in his heart for the troubles and sorrows of others.

Such afflictions make us better able to help others in trouble, and I have often thanked God as someone has left my study a happier person as a result of our talk together. This book will have been worth while if some in trouble or suffering take courage and seek God and their fellow men with renewed determination.

CHAPTER 11

Whose Responsibility?

MANY people can waste a great deal of energy, when they should be concentrating on getting well, trying to discover and argue as to who was responsible for their suffering. Their progress to health and back into the stream of life can be handicapped if they have wrong ideas on this subject of the responsibility of it all.

To rebuild your life again without the added canker of self-pity needs determination and courage, for the world is hard and is not going to make any allowances for you. There will be the odd people along the road who will be an encouragement and inspiration to you. They are the salt of the earth, and their savour is the Spirit of Christ which burns in their hearts even though they do not talk about it. Their light is set in a candlestick—like a city set on a hill for all to see.

The way you take suffering and rise above it with God's help will be a beacon of encouragement to others for God's glory. A beacon, like a lighthouse, has to have a firm foundation, so we have to have a correct basic understanding as to whose responsibility is cancer and suffering.

Some try very hard to "put up with suffering," as if God sends it and what God sends must be borne with pious subjection.

I am absolutely convinced from a study of God's word,

the Bible, and observation of life, that God, who is the perfect embodiment of love, does not send suffering. It is not willed by Him, the originator of all the forces of goodness. The smallest examination of life reveals that there is a great force of evil abroad—spiritually powerful and so cunningly diabolical in its directive that we give to the overruling mind behind it a personality.

Behind goodness we find the personality of God—nothing very creditable to understand that: little or no belief is required. But belief is required to accept the premises of Christianity, namely that Christ was God restricted in a human body and laid bare to the blasts of the forces of evil. Accept that, and many illuminating facets of God and His will for us are revealed.

Behind evil we find an undoubted personality inspiring it all, and for want of any other word we call that personality the devil. He is so shrewd that he does not want you to understand him or even believe in him, but he seeks to act through you, and he takes a fiendish delight in messing up our world and our lives. Much of our suffering comes as a direct result of our linking our wills with the devil and preferring his kind of apples, even if they give us a tummy ache. Unfortunately it is not always we who suffer as a result, but others.

For example, a disease may result from an immoral life and it may be passed on by a kiss to an innocent person. Innocent children may be born blind or deformed as a result many years later. God is not responsible for that: the immoral man is under the director general of evil—the devil. He and the devil are the originators of the sin, and sometimes the results are visible to our shame in this world, but this is not always so.

Punishment in this world does not always follow, for it is clear that many utterly evil and wicked men appear to escape their just deserts. But there is another world to come and a reckoning day for all, when the books will be opened as we all stand before the throne of God. Some will have Christ standing there as their advocate. Others will have none to plead for them.

Consider Revelation 20, verses 12–15:

I saw the dead, small and great, stand before God; and the books were opened; and another book was opened, which is the book of life; and the dead were judged out of those things which were written in the books, according to their works.

And the sea gave up the dead which were in it; and death and hell delivered up the dead which were in them; and they were judged every man according to their works.

And death and hell were cast into the lake of fire. This is the second death.

And whosoever was not found written in the book of life was cast into the lake of fire.

Returning for a moment to the evil-doing man in this world: it is unfortunate for us all that no man ever sins to himself alone but to his neighbour and to the world. The resultant evil that ensues may befall others who are completely innocent—a train wrecker injures many innocent travellers, an atom bomb kills many innocent people.

The law of consequences knows no evasions or omissions. God's requirements are lofty, as they make no concessions to evil. He gives no extra-special protection from the law of consequences to those who profess to be Christians.

The root of all sin is unbelief, and whereas a crime is the breaking of the laws of society, to sin is to break the indivisible law of God. Sin is that which we know to be wrong and yet do. Sin is that thing which mocks me when I want to live a better life. Sin is an attitude of mind which results in an act of the hand.

To commit a crime against the law may be daring, but to sin against love is dastardly, like the dog who bites his own master when he is being fed and fondled. God loves us—others love us.

No sin ever leaves us where it finds us; it always leaves some deposit behind, it obscures our vision, blunts the edge of the soul's refinement, weakens resistance to temptation, predisposes us to repeat the wrong, and affects the home we live in.

No man can be less than he ought to be without inflicting moral hurt upon the community, because every life increases the momentum of good or ill in the world.

Thousands suffer because they are part of a world which has been torn asunder by man down the course of history, and the evil nature is passed on from generation to generation.

A great deal of pain and suffering is the cumulative result of the wilful sin of man, which for generations has torn God's world apart. God does not send the bomb which blows your house to bits and kills or maims your family. God did not create the revolting German concentration camps and gas chambers. It is the world we have developed that has done it, and the instigators lined up against Christ two thousand years ago are alert right to this day.

An evil Herod glared over the shoulders of the Holy Child and has been glaring ever since, but God provided a way through the difficulty in the escape to Egypt, and He will provide a way for us.

He is not responsible for your pain and suffering but provides a way of living or even dying through it victoriously. We simply must get our thinking right and not blame Him, but claim the power to overcome—to take up our Cross in His strength and follow.

Suffering may indeed drive you to your knees, for, stripped of all the pleasures of life and faced with pain or suffering, what else can you and I hold on to but God? It is then that we often clear our minds of the clutter of life and surrender our very souls to Him, and find in Him a resting place; and even amid suffering He can make us glad.

Just because suffering or tragedy makes a person turn to God in desperation, it does not necessarily follow that the suffering was through the will of God and is designed for that person.

Search as we will, we will never find an adequate explanation as to why you or I have to go through a particular suffering while others appear to go through life scot-free. The only conclusion I can come to, apart from the absolute courting of disaster and trouble through one's own will, is that the rest of suffering comes as a result of our living in a world which has been disrupted by man. I think the most important thing is never to blame God for our suffering, never to become embittered about it but to be determined, individually, to rise above it and relieve the suffering of our fellow men.

Selfishness can increase the suffering of the world. A selfish man overlooks a thousand kindnesses of others, but never forgets the one kind deed he has done. He forgets his own thousand shortcomings, but makes a mountain out of any small failing in another.

We know only too well that man's inhumanity to man is something incredible and we should do our part to prevent this. To say or do nothing when righteousness is outraged is an act of betrayal. We should do our part to give courage to others and to rise above our own infirmities and disabilities. Without wallowing in corporate self-pity there is a strange sense of corporate courage which comes to us as we take our suffering to Him. The pagan world seems to go by, hale and healthy, with a "don't-care-a-damn" attitude, while the very Christ of God suffered.

We can enter into the fellowship of His suffering. It is as if we crawl from our bed to Calvary, caring not who sees, and cling to the foot of that Cross, sliding to the ground exhausted, but contented that He knows. Behind me I can feel the compassionate eyes of Mary, the mother, and all who down the centuries have made up the "fellowship of His suffering." Call it the communion of saints if you will, however unworthy we are to share in that company.

> Lift up your heads, O ye gates . . .
> and the King of Glory shall come in.

When the King of Glory comes into the citadel of my being as I am in the midst of suffering He helps me to "give with the pain" instead of resisting it; and this is the secret of enduring pain. I find that so much of pain is in the mind as well as the body, and it is the mind section of the pain which makes the other hurt the more. When I resent the pain and ask myself why it should be, then the volume of it increases and is harder to bear.

When I can yield and unite to God, the physical pain does not seem to hurt so much. I know this is true, for I have proved it so often, and it acts like medication, like a drug. It is food to the spirit which helps me to battle with the pain.

With the practice of the spiritual presence of God within, I go through a series of logical reasonings to try and get on top of the pain. I admit that these reasonings are not always logical. After a big operation there are bound to be convulsions of pain, for there are so many severed nerves inside—each looking round and seeking for its partner. I tell myself this and hope that the extra bout is due to the uniting of two nerves. And then it is a help to discuss it openly with my wife. I find I have to reduce things to a simple explanation in order to be able to dismiss it and not worry about it.

When the pain is really bad in the same old lumbar-pelvis regions, I say defiantly to myself: "What does it matter if I do die—but then it would be such a pity, for it would help to kill so many hopes which I have tried to instil into others. Oh, God, you cannot let that happen."

The mind begins to work on this problem of living and enjoying every minute, and I purposely undertake things which will take a long time to finish—just to spite myself. It helps to balance down the visions of my final farewell in my mind when I am depressed. Fear stalks around at such a time, for I know that medically I have only a 30-per-cent chance of living, once out of the hospital.

I see my wife's anxious face as she suffers the waiting period with me, and I know she is wondering if all this physical work and worry of the Greystoke adventure is good for me. But she knows I have a twofold policy—firstly to plan work which will take years to accomplish, thus indicating that I am counting on victory; and secondly to live in the present as if it is going to be my last battle for work and enjoyment.

It is a constant battle with fear, for over my head hangs the shadow of a secondary outbreak; but each day, week, or month increases the "odds" on my living and there is less likelihood of a second strike.

There have been some agonising periods when the lumbar and pelvis pains have been so bad that cancer of the bone was suspected. But the periods have passed, the clinical tests have proved negative, rheumatism or overstrain are diagnosed. Let me stress that fear adds to the pain, and when I have my mind and imagination under control through God, I can put up with the backache. When tempted to say I cannot go on, I take my battle to God, and in Him I gradually come to feel safe.

CHAPTER 12

A New Birth

THE phone rang by my bedside in the middle of the night, 3 A.M. It was Robert Young, the film actor, ringing up all the way from Beverly Hills to wish us good tidings and a happy New Year from his family and a group of friends who had gathered at his house.

How small the world is at such times! What a thrill it was for both of us to talk to them and live for a moment amongst these people from All Saints' Church, where Robert is a sidesman.

It is a pity more people do not realise that so many well-known stars like Robert, Glenn Ford, Barbara Britton, Spencer Tracy, Dale Evans, Roy Rogers, Raymond Massey and others are keen Christians and devoted to their churches.

Five months after my operation, on Christmas Day 1954, I began preaching once again at St. Michael's Church, Bournemouth. It was a moment of intense feeling for us as a family because, apart from practical and office work, it meant that I had begun my ministry again.

Behind the glad tidings and simplicity of that Christmas there were so many serious strands woven that my sense of gratitude to God for becoming a babe at Bethlehem was impregnated with a million other thoughts.

Behind the act of Christmas is the idea of a family home,

of peace with something to be pleased about, of a new spirit of giving and receiving. We had plenty to be pleased about.

By divine inspiration and by tradition, men gather in their homes with time off to be at leisure with their own in their own surroundings. Predominantly it is a children's feast, so grannies and grandpas and uncles come to where the children are. As we look back over the years, it is our childhood bedroom and home fireside that we remember with the Christmas decorations when we talk of home background. Tough luck on those without family circles and homes. Tough luck on you if Christmas finds you in a hospital bed, or if your home is broken up for one reason or another. As we learn "to give with pain" to ease its sting, so we must learn to unbend at Christmas time even if our lot is cast in a dark valley.

We look back at Mary and Joseph as they stand round that manger experiencing the supreme joy of this first-born Child, and there is the evil spirit of Herod hovering over their shoulders. Evil is present in that family amid their apparent peace and joy.

There is a fearful tug at Mary's heart and at Joseph's. She knew her Bible and all that had been prophesied for her Child—the Messiah of God.

Oh, there is more than the face of Herod: there is human sin—not just the fact that His own race are not going to receive Him. God's plan of redemption, ending on a cross with all its mystery, yet with a glorious resurrection, lies ahead.

If ever a mother or father ached over their child and future, they did. Mary's heart bled for the Child—she loved and she gave.

Don't we today? The younger ones who are married but as yet are without children. They are in love now, but when they watch together over their first child their love for one another will increase beyond their dreams. They will make sacrifices, but not as martyrs. They will stint and scrape to give that child the best, and will do it willingly.

But love and life are painful; there is a thorn in the very heart of it. No child ever grows up right of itself. No life ever surges on without pain. No character is built without constant rebirth. No soul is at peace until it finds its rest in God amid the bloody battlefield of life.

Mary and Joseph will have to do something more than stint and save, work and feed, love and teach. They must carry in their hearts God's terrible future for their Child. They have to help Him to do the will of God. They have to be in the background.

To them Christmas was a serious business as well as a joyful one.

Behind my wife's cheerful face I know she carries a burden in her heart over me that I am unable to remove.

During the thirteen years that I was vicar in Aylesbury, I saw many things in the school of life, but none stand out so vividly as an emergency baptism at Christmas time. The doctor, the mother, and I knew that the child could not live very long, even if it survived the first few years. Amid the joy of a newborn child, the mother was in chronic anguish.

Mary knew her Boy would ride out into the world and claim all men and women as His brothers and sisters.

It would be human if His mother was hurt by the warmth of a love that could give to others and to the world as He gave to her. Do you remember the incident? He claimed all men as His brother or mother.

All parents feel that kind of pang when their child falls in love. The foolish, selfish parent pretends his or her heart is broken or seeks to be possessive: but life must go on—it cannot stand still. The wise parent takes the girl of their son's choice and accepts her "in the beloved"—in other words, because the girl is precious to the son and the son is precious to his parents she is accepted in the son.

"Unto us who believe He is precious," and we know that Christ is the incarnate Son of God. We read with new meaning at Christmas time those famous words in the Bible: "To the praise of the glory of His grace wherein He hath made us accepted in the beloved." (Ephesians 1:6) The Babe of Bethlehem was the dearest possible possession to Mary, but she had to share Him with the world. It is in the going on and the losing that there is pain. But for Mary, He was not to be lost to another single person but He was to be shared with many other people and then to die.

How could she bear it except by believing in Him? If ever He was received, it was by Mary. Right to the Cross. How can we bear suffering except by believing in Him?

She had loved God so much as a girl that she bore His Son. She loved that Son so much as a mother that she withdrew to the shadows and gave Him to the world. It was her life she gave—without her, God could not have had a human body in which He could suffer and be tempted in all points as we are. She gave to God a human voice He could speak with and tell of Himself. She gave to God a body to be crucified on Calvary.

We might well have shrunk from such a task—*but she gave*. That is the first Christmas giving—the giving of oneself. She lived deep and so must we. Her very giving supplied her desire for life while her receiving of Him gave the power to live and be a child of God.

What is all this to us?

A reminder to be emptied of self and receive Him in our hearts. "He came unto His own, and His own received Him not. But as many as received Him to them gave He power to become the sons of God."

Have you opened the door of your heart to the coming

of Christ into the very citadel of your being? Nicodemus, who came to Jesus by night, was told he had to be born again spiritually, inside. The miracle of Bethlehem had to take place in his heart, not by might nor by power, but by the very Spirit of a living God.

This is the crux of Christianity: the miracle of faith—for faith in its essence is God's work in your heart. As a babe quickens in the womb of a mother and she knows the assurance of the new life within, so the new birth essential to a Christian quickens his soul.

Have you received Him? If you have, you will know your birthright: "Power to become the sons of God." You are not on your own—He has bought you back. You then have a new lease of life and this carries new responsibilities and will gradually change your perspective. It is the expulsive power of a new affection, and I confess that since cancer has knocked on my door I have found a new affection for life. I see things and people through different eyes, and I long to bring spiritual help and courage to others.

I cannot express in words how grateful I am to God for this extension of life, and how much more I appreciate, all around me.

CHAPTER 13

Living on Borrowed Time

A YEAR ago today, I had my operation, and at times America seems such a long way off, although I have had many Americans to stay at Greystoke, and look back on a year of ceaseless activity during which much has been created and wild dreams have been made to come true. Despite the repeated warnings by doctors, I am sure that the preoccupation has been the best thing for me, because it would have been all too easy to retire to bed and feel desperately sorry for myself with each crescendo of pain.

From my bedroom window I look out over one of the most fabulous views in almost all England. It takes your breath away for sheer beauty, and in fact nothing even in the South of France or California can equal it.

In the distance are the purple Purbeck Hills, surrounding the colourful basin of Poole Harbour, one of the largest natural harbours of the world, dotted with little emerald islands amid the deep blue of the sea. Vivid splashes of green spartina grass and yellow sandy beaches glisten in the sun. This is the Riviera of England.

Looking left over the narrow neck of land called Sandbanks is the English Channel and the white cliffs of the Old Harry Rocks coast line. Beyond is the Isle of Wight.

This sleepy harbour, with its attractive creeks and four tides a day, is a paradise for all kinds of boats and yachts, and as I sit up in bed writing this I am fascinated by the multitude of yachts and motor cruisers riding at anchor with their graceful white hulls gleaming in the early-morning sun. The whole view is draped with pine trees, and there is even a tall palm tree in our garden to remind me of California.

Into this natural harbour sailed the Danes and Romans two thousand years ago, to be followed by ships of the Spanish Armada. Here they practised burning oil on the sea to frighten the Germans from invading, and later staged the D-Day rehearsals. But now all is calm again, and the large vista speaks peace to those who have eyes to see. Such a view and reminder of God's wonderful handiwork in nature does something to one's soul, and I feel daily the thrill of being alive.

Boats are like humans: they are built to ride out the rough patches of life with the storms and strong tides, and it is amazing what they will stand up to before they sink.

At night the scene changes, and during the long hours of a sleepless night I watch the winking lights of the buoys which mark the channel. Their regular blinking lights are a companionship in the night—friendly reminders in the darkness that they are there to do a job of work to guide others past the sandbanks. They remind me that my life must be a beacon to others, for no man lights a candle and hides it under a bushel, but puts it in a candlestick for all to see, like a city set on a hill, so that it cannot be hidden.

I pray that God will grant me time in life to light the way for others who suffer, past the sandbanks of surrender, defeat and self-pity. The way is not to look up to others, for all of us humans are so very frail and fallible, and if people were to pin their faith on fellow mortals they would so easily be let down.

Faith must be pinned on one who is higher than our-

selves, and the winking lights of the friends of God must
mark the clear, deep channel which leads to God and thus
to human happiness and courage.

I well remember Pastor Martin Niemöller telling me,
while we were in Amsterdam in 1949, how his great concern when in a Nazi concentration camp was to keep a
light burning for God in Dachau. There is an opportunity
for you to be true and brave right at your very door. Do
not let us be blinded by propinquity.

As to the physical side, by the seventh and eighth week
after my operation I was able to drive the car, though it
was not exactly comfortable—but at least I was not so de-
pendent on others. The hospital had taught will power and
muscle control over the wretched colostomy, and even by
the third week I had considerable control—and soon the
control was virtually complete. It is extraordinary what
you can teach the body to do. Weeks will go smoothly by
with the regular hour each morning in the bathroom to
adjust the tube, which I fully admit is quite a daily ordeal,
requiring a determined mental adjustment to life. This part
can be very painful, and it may not go according to plan,
but for those who fear it I would like to say:

"It's not really so dreadful, though at times you may wish
to roll up and die. Come to work it all out, it is so much
better than dying, and life is jolly good. Count up the good
things continually. Do not take aspirin or opium if you cannot control your body with your mind. Find out more about
methylcellulose.

A woman quickly forgets the pain of labour for the joy
that a child is born: so you will forget the pain for the joy
that you are still alive and there is so much to do in life.

While I was in hospital this was the part I loathed, and
it was so thundering painful that I dreaded the daily round
which was to be my lot for the rest of my life. So today
every time I feel like complaining when the whole proce-

dure is particularly painful, I throw myself on my bed, have a good groan to myself, clutch a hot-water bottle, and try to remember that the pain will go, that God is in His heaven and that the rest of the twenty-four hours have fun and excitement in them. It is nice to be alone at such a time, though what I would do without my wife I just do not know. She guesses when I have a pain or am battling with a wave of depression and comes to my rescue.

I think courage is not something that you put on at high moments in your life, but something that you have to sweat out alone with God, day by day. Sufferings should be steppingstones, not stumbling blocks, and so I pray and battle with God for strength, for He says that His strength is made perfect in our weakness. I am a weak vessel for Him to fill. So I find that gradually the pains go. I am all right again. I repeat to myself almost like a gramophone: "I'm jolly lucky to be alive and the pain is going." And do you know, it does! The power of positive thinking is something to be practised, and it is really extraordinary what you can will yourself to do if you set your mind to it.

To fellow patients, let me say: "I don't bother to diet for the colostomy, for that would be such a fag and a bore for others." In fact I eat like a horse, anything and everything, until there is a rebellion, though I will admit it is easier if one does not eat too much. I live such an energetic life, painting our house, gardening, sawing down trees, office work, preaching and sailing, that I feel I need the extra calories of a manual worker.

Life is too short to mess about being an invalid: it's bad enough to have to cope with one's restrictions, let alone fiddling around with a diet, for that would make one conscious all the time that life was different.

I feel that the great thing for cancer or polio people is to make life feel as normal as possible, with plenty of work to be done, so that we can conquer our disabilities lest the great evil of self-pity gets encouragement.

Some people, when they are ill, like you to commiserate with them till they wallow in self-pity and your visit depresses them rather than cheers them up. To strike the happy medium between this and appearing to treat their trouble too lightly is a tricky problem. During my time as a hospital chaplain I had plenty of opportunity to experience the task of sitting by a person's bed to give them sympathy and yet encouragement. After the bombing blitz on London, the wards were full of poor unfortunate people for whom one's heart bled—in one bed might be a waitress and in the next a duchess. In pain the rich and poor are met together; God is the Father of them all, and we are His stewards to bring them hope and courage.

Sympathy and understanding is communicated not so much by words, but by your hand in theirs, a look and a prayer. It is a gift for which we need to ask God's help, for we know how important courage and the will to live is to the patient, and they must feel that someone cares for them in the spiritual sense and is expecting the best from them. It is a disservice to pander to their self-pity and it is not easy to strike a balance.

What you do for others in kindness cannot be measured in terms of hours of work or rates of pay, or it will choke you. You pass through this world but once, and if you can turn the blind eye to suffering and injustice, then you must write yourself down as despicable, selfish, and unworthy of anyone's help when your time of need comes. It is not enough to write out a cheque for a money gift.

When I wake in the morning and lie in bed, sometimes every ache in my body comes to my conscious mind as if my spine and pelvis were going to split apart. To search for a cause gets me no further, so the only thing to do is to get up and start moving about.

Likewise, to lie back and wait to know God's will brings every doubt to your conscious mind, but the only thing to do in the situation, having committed yourself to God, is to be up and doing, trusting that God will work His way out with you. Yes, to me it is a strange mixture of faith, courage, and Christianised common sense, constantly mellowed by the events of life. Some people talk glibly of the guidance of God and claim all their decisions are of His guidance, whereas really and truly this is only an impudent way of boosting their own ego.

Because the problem of God's guidance and share of our lives is so vast and complex, we might be tempted not to bother Him about the little things—the day-to-day things —yet these are the very things we need Him for, they are our very daily bread. There are moments to me when I need His daily bread, for the uplift of my spirit, more than all the physical things around me, for it would be an unbalanced picture to pretend that by being fantastically busy, all is always well.

I think it is perfectly extraordinary how tactless people are: time and time again, when they know you have had cancer, they immediately trot out some ghastly gruesome story of someone they knew who died this way or that from it. One of these days I think I shall stop them short, in high hopes that they will learn a lesson and spare some other sufferer.

It is bad enough to have to keep your own end up and pretend to yourself that you are not worried as to whether every new ache is not cancer all over again, without their garbled, colourful account. The Dismal Desmonds of this life are notorious, and they usually unload on the wrong people. People add bits to make their story more spicy— not content to see that you are putting up a good face, they proceed to broadcast what is bound to downcast. In imaginary sympathy, they describe conditions worse than yours purposely in the mistaken idea that you will take courage that your fate is not as bad as that.

There are thoughtless people who do not know the meaning of sympathy and encouragement. I have a prayer which runs like this: "O God, give me the gift of sympathy that I may help others, and guard me from clumsiness. Give me eyes to see so that I may weep with those who weep and rejoice with those who do rejoice. Use me if it is possible to make happy and strong the hearts of others and humbly to set forth Thy light, which is the light of the world. Amen."

No two cases are ever the same, but I do know of some cancer colostomy cases who relax and resign themselves to become chronic invalids staying in bed all the time. To me that is utterly defeatist.

Between periods of rest I sometimes work fourteen or fifteen hours a day and love it, and only wish I had twice the strength to match my energy. There is so much to do in life and so little time left in which to do it that I feel I must crowd as much in as possible with periodical checkups by X ray and blood sedimentation-rate tests.

My daughter, Susan, is now aged twelve and she has just gone to her public school as a boarder. It was a tremendous joy to help buy her new grown-up clothes and uniform, and it was to me one of the joys of living. Now I want to live long enough to see her through school and then happily married! Then, I expect, I will want to see my grandchildren. Oh, there is so much to live for, and life becomes so much more exciting and valuable when you have nearly lost it and when each month lived through increases the assurance of a longer life.

Do you know that kind of tug at your heart when you kiss a child goodbye at the beginning of a term at a new boarding school? Often you feel it more than the child, who eagerly looks forward to meeting new friends and to finding out which dormitory and bed she is to have. You suddenly feel for her all the pain of growing up, of homesickness, of petty bullies and a million pinpricks.

As I look out on all those I love—wife, children, black Scottie dog, and friends—I long with all my heart that God will grant me more time. I thank **God** for a ruthless surgeon and pray that no secondary **attack** may ever break out to rob me of all the dear things of life, family, and home.

Some people have told me that they would commit suicide if they had cancer, or that they would not struggle to live. I find there is so much to live for, as you can see, and I try to remind myself of these things when I have a few off days. I feel I owe it to fellow cancer patients to keep my end up and be a source of encouragement to them. Besides I value life, work, and people so much more now, and to me it is colossal fun to create something out of Greystoke—the vast mansion I bought by cable at the time of my operation. There is nothing like real hard work to take your mind off yourself and your aches and pains.

CHAPTER 14

A Wagon to the Stars

By now it must be clear, even to the most casual reader, that my dream castle, which helped to sustain me while in hospital, has become almost a matter of life and death to me. I am even more in love with it and its possibilities than I was when I first set eyes on it three or more years ago. Strange how houses can play so large a part in our lives and assume a personality of their own. I rather like the idea of the world to come which Jesus gave us when he said, "In my Father's house are many rooms." It gives me the idea that if you are going to feel stuffy in the drawing room you can wander along to another room. I preach in so many different churches and within a few moments I know whether that church is warm and receptive. Quickly I feel at home and it becomes easy to preach where a church has been prayed and worshipped in by real people.

So it is with houses, for some people's homes are cold and cheerless, however well they may be furnished. "Where no oxen are the crib is clean." Everything is neat and tidy and there is no patter of little feet along the passages, no spontaneous friendships round the fireside.

These things do not just happen—they grow with the laughter, sweat, and tears of those who live in the home. Although people are of supreme importance, I think it is right that we humans should give our homes as much at-

tention as we can, and what fun it is to decorate a house
and fashion it to fit the personality of your family.

Come to our home—Greystoke—and you will first be
greeted by a friendly black Scottie curled up in the sun outside the front door. It is no trouble at all to him to uncurl
and literally frivol all round you, grinning up the side of his
mouth, and giving a series of sneezes as a welcome. Perfectly ridiculous, but it is nice—utterly useless as a burglar
alarm unless you have a black poodle with you. Step inside
the house and you are immediately enchanted with its
magnificent oak panelling, shining mahogany doors, and
above all the breath-taking view over the pine trees, of the
most perfect natural harbour in the world. "It just isn't
true," my friends will so often say. "How on earth did you
find such a paradise in so lovely a setting. It's a dream, but
what on earth are *you* doing with it?" They then wander
round admiring the blue swimming pool, the furnishings,
and the ultramodern décor.

I have to explain that it is a wild dream that we have
literally *made* come true, but not without immense work
and a good deal of financial worry. If I had come home
to England after four weeks in an American hospital and
convalesced for a year, twiddling my thumbs waiting for a
secondary attack, I would have gone off my head. I had to
work and hitch my wagon to the furtherest star. Work takes
your mind off yourself and your problems, so it is most
important for anyone in trouble to find a job which is completely absorbing.

My interest in Greystoke began during Holy Week 1954
when I ended up my series of missions in churches in many
cities with a whole week's film mission in the Winter
Gardens, Bournemouth. This is one of the finest concert
halls in Britain, seating sixteen hundred people, and I used
a twenty-five-foot plastic screen with a 16-mm. projector.
The film was called *I Beheld His Glory,* and the mission

was backed by the united churches of the town, including Roman Catholics. Many professed that it marked a turning point in their lives, either as this first contact with the Christian message or as a rededication of their lives. We use films for challenging evangelism and not as a picture luxury for the already religious.

A record number of 12,500 people attended, and on the closing day, in response to an expression of appreciation from the clergy, I thanked the people of Bournemouth and Poole for their wonderful support of the Film Crusade. In a kind of "end-of-term" speech I accidentally let slip that one day I would like to move my Dawn Trust quarters to Bournemouth, if ever I could find a suitable building, for I had so many roots in the area.

The next morning various house agents rang me up offering all sorts of properties which were being sold. I explained that it was only a chance remark and that Dawn Trust was not ready to move from its studio at Aylesbury and, besides, we were always broke for we had no wealthy sponsor and I was leaving for America in four days' time.

Lord Lyle, the famous sugar king, had recently died and his secretary rang up and offered me his lovely mansion of Greystoke and said I could have it for a "song." I had known Lord Lyle and had often admired his house, so it was rather like being offered Buckingham Palace!

When I inspected it closely I fell completely in love with it—hook, line, and sinker, but the so-called song was a cool £27,000, which was about half its original cost. The price, which included a great deal of extra land for building sites, was quite out of the question. The house in its superb position was unique in all England. The setting was more enchanting than anything in the Mediterranean; in fact it was too good to be used merely as a film headquarters.

My mind raced on to ideas of a residential conference house, but I had to turn down the whole suggestion. "I

admit I am in love with the place," I told the secretary
and his agent, "but I leave for America on Thursday and I
haven't any money. If you can sell off some of the land and
give me the house for next to nothing, that would be grand.
I will leave you my various addresses in America." Admittedly the house was a glorious dream, fit for the most inspiring rendezvous.

As we crossed America cables flashed to-and-fro as the
price dropped from £27,000 to £20,000 . . . £15,000 . . .
£10,000 until it finally reached £8000 a few days before
I collapsed with cancer. I presumed they had sold off all
the extra land and tennis courts as building sites, which
indeed had been done.

At this moment we were pleading with God for an extension of life and I firmly believed that He was going to
answer our prayers. I argued with myself: "Why not act as
if you believed God and really were going to live." A little
voice inside me seemed to be prodding me on, saying,
"Greystoke would be a big enough target, hitch your
wagon to the highest star and go for it." Then at this critical moment my surgeon challenged me that I must be *determined to live,* so I asked myself how better could I prove
my determination than by sending that extraordinary cable to my friend in England, telling him to buy the house.
Yes, it was indeed an emotional decision . . . was it
bravado? Was it to prove to myself that I believed God
would let me live?

While I lay in hospital the house became to me a symbol
of my determination to live, but little did I realise what I
was letting myself in for. I stuck the picture of the house
on the wall and my American friends just could not believe that I had bought such a fabulous house for the sum
of £8000 ($24,000) which would hardly buy a chicken
coop in Beverly Hills, let alone a house with a Grecian
swimming pool.

It seemed easy to raise this sum while still breathing the rarefied air of California, where money for business or charity flows so easily.

My wife stood by me magnificently, clutching at any straw which might encourage me to live. I know now that she trembled at this vast undertaking with the critical time which lay ahead. Wisely, she said nothing, while I was in hospital, to kill my spirits and enthusiasm for something which seemed to buoy me up and give me an absorbing interest.

The moment I set foot in England my time of testing came, for I had to find the capital quickly to complete the purchase, and the rose-coloured spectacles I was wearing in Hollywood lay broken on the ground.

On our way from the hospital in London to my cottage, we visited the house. To see it bare, empty and stripped of all its furniture, was a sorry sight. Catrin saw it for the first time and quaked in her shoes, pointing out some of the snags. "See where all the pictures have been. We will have to paint all the walls before anyone sees it or no one will help us finance it." "We will do it ourselves," I said to keep my courage up, knowing that we hadn't any money.

According to the contract, the completion date for the purchase of Greystoke had been fixed for the end of October, so from the moment I arrived at my water's-edge cottage on the isolated Goathorn Peninsula on September first I was frantic to raise at least the purchase price of £8000. It is not easy to raise £100 in life, at a moment when you desperately need it, let alone £8000 and more. I looked out of my cottage window watching many a glorious sunrise reveal the long stretch of water inside the harbour, dotted with boats, and there I could see my dream castle, sitting majestically on the sky line. I remembered how the late Lord Lyle had got out his enormous yacht in order to steam over to my birthday party only the year before. His great yacht, with its towering funnel and glistening white paint, had dwarfed all the other yachts, even a visiting American millionaire's boat which had dropped anchor off our little pier.

Funny how money comes easily to some people and how money just goes on making more money in some people's hands. Yet, here I was, brimful of ideas for the future, desperate for someone to back me. I tackled, by phone and by letter, every conceivable bank and person in the frantic rush against time, without success, yet every day the sun would reveal that challenging house on the edge of Canford Cliffs.

One of my directors of Dawn Trust rang me and explained how glad he was to have me alive and back in England, but, "Please give up this crazy idea of Greystoke which I read about in the national newspapers . . . it is bound to fail . . . I am only thinking of you and Catrin." (My directors are good friends and unpaid.) He, Canon Bryan Green, insisted that I call a meeting of all the directors and advisers for October fifteenth. Obviously I had to find the money somehow by then, or they would insist that I gave up the whole idea.

There are many famous people on the Dawn Trust list of patrons, but their gifts to this particular work were for the most part a five-pound note and the use of their names. I had already exhausted my own money, for during my years of pioneering religious films I had already loaned to the Trust some £12,000 of my own money without interest, because I believe in the spiritual value of work. Part of this money was my remuneration for designing caravans for postwar aircraft companies.

I kept telling myself: "Surely there must be someone with money who can see that not only is Greystoke an incredible bargain, but has enormous possibilities. . . . How can I reach that one person?"

I believe in going straight to the fountainhead, so I tried
the directors of my bank, but without success. I tackled
Air Commodore Hellmore, head of Castor R and many
other firms, but Bill was his usual gay and charming self
and left me with a feeling that it would be easy to find the
money and suggested people I should see. On the way
over to America on the *Queen Mary*, I had talked with
Lord Rothermere, over a few drinks, of the potentialities
of Greystoke as a leadership training centre, but now when
I wanted him he was in the West Indies. I suggested that
one of the things we could do at Greystoke would be to run
a school for sailing for boys to be sponsored by the *Daily
Express*, to my old school friend Max Aitken, who had
succeeded his father as head of the Beaverbrook Press. He
was genuinely keen on the idea . . . hopes ran high, but
such a project would take time and did eventually go the
way of many bright ideas. So I went from pillar to post to
find any kind of sponsor and the completion date and the
board meeting drew nearer.

My friend to whom I had sent the fateful telegram came
over in his speedboat to see me almost every day and this
Jim Carey Wood, who himself was always full of easy
happy-go-lucky ideas, would sit for hours on the terrace,
looking over the water, discussing how we could beat this
thing.

"I've an idea, for what it is worth. You may not know it,
but there is a new branch of a Lancashire milling bank from
the North of England, called Williams Deacon's Bank,
opening in Bournemouth in October and they want cus-
tomers and they might . . . well you never know."

"But, my dear old Jim, they would not start a new branch
by loaning bags of gold!" As I said this I could see that he
was quite serious about it.

"The manager has already advanced a great deal to certain local business concerns, and Dawn Trust has not only

a national name but a great following in Bournemouth. You could change your bank to his. I will get him to meet you at the house and you do your stuff."

It was almost too good to be true, for the manager was just about the most charming person you could ever meet and he fell in love with the house and seemed to be swept on by my enthusiasm. I asked for £8000 for the house in return for the deeds, and £2500 for alterations and repairs against my own personal guarantee, for what that was worth. I warned him that I might die any minute and that others were afraid to help a fellow who had had a miracle operation for cancer.

Four days later the phone rang. "My directors in Manchester have graciously authorised me to advance you the money." The joy was terrific, in fact too much so to worry about how long it would take to pay it back, or to realise that it would cost three times as much for alterations and furnishing. I looked forward to seeing the faces of my co-directors at the coming board meeting. The meeting was a great success and the purchase of the house was unanimously approved.

Words can never convey the anguish that went on in my mind concerning the financial side of this new project. I was loath to give up the house even though my fellow directors and bishop patrons of my Dawn Trust were still alarmed at the magnitude of the task of raising so much money as well as the money for alterations, furnishing, and running. They were concerned that the task would not only kill me but drag down my life's work. But gradually they too became fascinated with this lovely mansion and advised me to seek advice from experienced businessmen.

My good friend, Arthur Rank, whom I had helped to push into the film business, wrote me a charming letter of welcome home to Britain and to life. But he went on to say that he had heard I had bought Lord Lyle's house and

begged me to give it up, saying it was too big a job for a
sick man.

I was convinced it was God's will, though it is always so
very difficult to distinguish between what is one's own desire and what is God's. Maybe some would call it a spiritual
hunch about a house which I saw in general terms as a
rendezvous for all kinds of people where they could come
for holidays, for conferences to discuss subjects of mutual
interest, and to gain inspiration for the rough ways of life.
A rendezvous for those in need of change, to come and
renew their courage and determination to face life and help
others. A residential clubhouse for all who were interested
in my Dawn Trust with its films and international fellowship.

We tried not to spend anything of the redecoration
money, and so occupied all the first winter months on the
end of ladders, painting the house ourselves from top to
bottom. In this we had the help of two yachting friends
who came with their rollers to help with the endless walls.
The wallpapering and electric wiring and suchlike began to
take shape, but the most boring part was the making of
miles of curtains for the many huge windows. Our sewing
machine worked overtime.

At night we would drop into bed, utterly worn out, almost too tired to talk or even think of the possibility of
death or failure, but it was fun creating something. I was
more than ever convinced that, one way or another, the
house would succeed in the long run and God would let
me live. My wife came round to this way of thinking, and
whenever money worries came up we tried to convince ourselves that if only the bank would give us time, the project would succeed.

The shadow of the bank manager became more menac-
ing when the credit squeeze was ordered by the govern-
ment, and I think it required just as much courage to keep

the bank at bay as it did to live as if I had no disabilities
and as if no secondary could ever happen. Our business
advisors told us that it would be quite impossible to find
sponsors, however worthy the objective might be. We were
advised on all hands to run it on the lines of a very elegant
hotel, at least in the summer season, or else give up the
house and the dreams. Thus by a steady flow of visitors and
members we would create a bread-and-butter line to pay
the rates and maybe "carry" the low-fee paying conferences
which never take place in the height of the summer season.
Residence at what you might call the clubhouse of Dawn
Trust would not be a closed shop, but open to all. Even the
casual holiday and overseas visitors would soon notice and
enjoy the difference about Greystoke.

Few of the people who have visited Greystoke for conferences or for their holidays guess the struggles and risks
which went on behind the scenes. On the one hand there
were the prophets of doom, who warned me that without a
sponsor it would be quite impossible to adapt, furnish, and
establish Greystoke as a conference house or hotel. They
said I would go bankrupt and have a nervous breakdown
into the bargain.

On the other hand, there were the few optimistic friends
who not only believed in us but thought that Greystoke
was such an enchanting house in such an unparalleled position that it could not fail. Our backs were to the wall and
the situation at times was desperate, for no sponsor could
be found. I had dreamed that Greystoke would be such a
success that it would soon sponsor my religious-film work,
but the alterations and furnishings were costing nearly as
much as the purchase price.

Only one man, apart from Williams Deacon's Bank, gave
me any sizeable material help and he was a Greek shipping
millionaire, Stavros Niarchos. My trip to St. Moritz was
not really a matter of pleasure, but to keep an appointment

with him. He had helped me once before in my life, but no one finances a condemned man! When you are known to have had extensive cancer, people look at you in a queer way as if you ought not to be alive and are going to drop down dead any minute. So I skied down his Niarchos runs for which he had just donated a million Swiss francs, and the idea was to show him that there was life in the old dog yet. The Earl of Warwick warned me not to ask for too little, explaining that Niarchos did not understand small figures.

Holding on to my seat, I casually asked for £50,000 to cover not merely Greystoke but all my film projects. He did not bat an eyelid, but said he hoped I did not want him to decide there and then.

Naturally, I did, and explained that I understood that every really big businessman knows within five minutes of an interview whether he is going through with a project presented to him by someone, irrespective of the details.

We had a laugh over this, but I did not get my request. Instead I received a gift of £250 with a promise that it would be annual. Being Mr. Niarchos, he has been true to his word.

This one helping hand gave me more encouragement than the value of the cheque, and it prevented me from wasting time looking for illusive sponsors. I must create something—prove it to be a going and attractive concern—and then maybe someone would help it to go places. We rolled up our sleeves and put on our artistic thinking caps in order to create the kind of attractive décor which you would expect to find in a Hollywood home. I remember being overwhelmed by the décor of the Orson Welles/Rita Hayworth homestead in Beverly Hills which had to be seen to be believed.

The floor of our sitting room was constantly littered with house-fashion magazines, yards of curtaining, sample bits

of futurist wallpaper, and the inevitable sewing machine.
The décor "war" is still going on and I begin to doubt if
it will ever finish. The bedrooms, some with private bath-
rooms, are all done in the same modern contemporary
style, with delicate blue candlewick bedspreads. Only one
looks as if Picasso had been let loose around the walls, and
it may serve to cheer someone up.

Talking of artists, although my wife paints landscapes
she refuses to try her hand on murals except with a
common-or-garden paintbrush. To overcome this difficulty
and to create something different, we have papered the
walls a deep red in the nautical room, where there is a
life-size specially made boat. The ceiling is blue with
white stars resembling the milky way and on the red walls
a friend of mine who is an artist for *Punch* has drawn
nautical caricatures.

All this may sound quite crazy inside so magnificent a
house, but I believe there is room in our world for a hotel-
conference house—call it what you will—that is different. I
enjoy making people happy, comfortable, and at ease to
talk to one another, and this compensates for a great deal
of hard work. We never set out to work so hard and it is
never possible to look into the future, but apart from the
amusement we get out of it there is a serious side, and at
least we have been able to create a hotel which is the envy
of all who stay there.

At Whitsun 1955 it was ready, and as the Bishop of
Jarrow, John Ramsbotham, was staying with us he dedicated it for its threefold purpose: a headquarters for the
Dawn Trust, a conference house, and a hotel. With
the most brilliant weather England has had in years, the
guests poured in from all parts of Britain, as well as from
America and Europe. We augmented the staff by employ-
ing university students, choosing those who were confessed
members of the Church. We hope that everything is a good

witness to the integrity of the Christian tradition without forcing religion on those who come. Greystoke has an inspirational atmosphere all its own.

In Greystoke I have a wonderful lookout circular tower room at the top of the house. From its windows I can see above the trees out to sea to the Isle of Wight, Studland Bay, and back over Poole Harbour to the blue Purbeck Hills. It is an uplifting sight at any time. This is my chapel in the sky, and when I celebrate Holy Communion there for my staff and guests, I feel more especially the uplifting power of the communion of saints.

It is well known that to run any residential establishment is extremely hard work at the best of times, especially with every possible room occupied for the whole summer season, so we found ourselves working flat out.

We were determined to make a success of it, for on this depended our ability to create a new type of hotel, conference house, and headquarters for Dawn Trust. We know what we like to find at an ideal hotel in the way of comfortable beds, good food, and many other things, and we resolved that Greystoke should have these things and build a good reputation for a unique hotel and we held a series of parties to introduce people to each other.

The whole thing went with a swing, everyone seemed to enjoy themselves tremendously, and we ended the first season with a house full of Members of Parliament. In fact, from every angle, the entire venture was a huge success, and we reduced the capital overdraft on the complete undertaking. I have learned far more about human nature and the handling of people than I ever thought possible, even after thirteen years as a vicar.

Our first conference was arranged by a very old friend with whom I shared so many adventures in our youth up at Cambridge. He—Joost de Blank—is now Bishop of Stepney in London and he had the bright idea of inviting all his rural deans and their wives to Greystoke for a three-day "get-together" and conference in January 1956. We had to call in staff, because we were closed for alterations. The workmen, indeed, only left three days before the conference began, but the conference was a success. The Reverend St. John Groser and other clergy celebrated Holy Communion each morning in the chapel in the tower.

We opened officially for 1956 at Easter with a houseful, and this was followed by a Dawn Trust house party and a conference for the Free Church Federal Council. Bournemouth, as far as hotels are concerned, is a seasonal place and claims to be the premier seaside resort of England, enjoying the most sunshine, and Canford Cliffs, where Greystoke is situated, is the residential end. What Beverly Hills is to Los Angeles, and Los Angeles to America, so is this part to England. It is, indeed, an ideal place to stay in order to enjoy the beauty of the southern part of England, being only thirty miles from Southampton. Oxford, Bath, Glastonbury, Salisbury, and Plymouth are all within striking distance. Once again during our second season we had a steady flow of holiday visitors from Britain, Europe, and America, and we were awarded a classification of three stars from the Royal Automobile Club and the Automobile Association. We had been a little afraid that our first year's success was beginner's luck, but the success of the second year proved the future possibilities. Although a new undertaking needs at least four or five years to establish itself on really firm foundations, it is tremendously encouraging that a wild dream has come true and that Greystoke is a resounding success, and that the overdraft at the bank has been greatly reduced. The hotel side fortunately only operates between Easter and the end of September, just when our film work is at its lowest ebb. And although we miss all the happy people, we are glad when the season ends, and by this time we are plotting and planning the

religious-film programs which go out during the winter
months to thousands of churches and Sunday schools.
Greystoke also gives office space to my work in the field of
cancer relief.

The success of Greystoke is, in no small measure, due to
my wife, who has worked with me and bravely held her
breath as she watched me shoulder more and more work.
She worries over any new pain I may have, wondering
whether it is a secondary outbreak arriving to strike me
down. She knows how much I have staked on this decision,
in a Los Angeles hospital, to buy Greystoke. She is so very
much part of my determination to live and she realises that
for me to live involves a desire to create as well as to enjoy
life to the full. When time may be short, every moment
and every day is of great value.

When she married me and took over the job of looking
after a sick man and bringing up my two children, little
did she realise how great a task it was to become. It is never
easy for any stepmother to win the respect and later the
love of young children who have for some time come to
regard their father's love as their exclusive possession. It is
important to make children feel part of a family where
loyalty to every member of the household is vital to the
security of the home.

It has given me great pleasure, over the years, to watch
her building a solid friendship with them as equals—never
pressing for love or any return for the million unselfish
things which we grownups do for our children.

I have never spanked either of my children and I believe that one sows good seeds for their characters if they
continually see a parent's unselfishness, generosity, and un-
stinted service of them. I know that some say: "It is not
worth it. Children are never grateful and unless you are
tough with them they will always take everything for
granted and will never learn to give anything in return."

I do not believe this philosophy and I must take this risk of building the right ideas into my children even if at the end they trample underfoot the love and affection of their home. Anyway, it is not gratitude we want from our children but love and real fellowship which always respects the growing individuality of each one of them. Without knowing it, the greatest joy which my children give to me is when they go to my wife first to recount their doings and to explain the things they have found in the garden or on the beach.

It takes a big heart and much patience to love someone else's children, for reserve has to play so large a part and there is the ever-present risk of being hurt. "Love ever stands with open hands and while it lives it gives." So Catrin has, for years, been the backbone of our home—the best critic of my sermons—and following hard on the heels of our American experience, where the blow of cancer fell, has come the added responsibility of running a very top-grade residential country house by the sea.

This involves controlling staff, catering, wages, and designing menus for five-course meals. The diplomas she gained at her finishing school, so long ago, have at last come in useful, for she was not anxious to hand over to a manageress.

Life certainly takes some strange turns for most of us, but hard work never killed anyone. Amongst the many things we have in common there is one particular thing which absorbs us both and that is our love for Greystoke, its view, its atmosphere, and the pleasure it gives to us and others.

CHAPTER 15

Talking of Cancer

"WHAT causes cancer?" This is a question I have so often been asked nowadays in a kind of confidential manner, as if I had found out the secret. But the truth is that no one really knows, despite all the cancer research that has gone on in Britain, America, and elsewhere.

Naturally, quite a number of things are known about it, and I have made it my business, since my operation, to find out as much as I can about cancer and what is being done for suffering humanity. For example, *cancer is neither catching nor proved to be hereditary.* There are predispositions in certain families to bodily imbalance which can be regarded as a weakness if illness should come their way.

I am appalled by the fact that a vast number of people who appear perfectly healthy and not the least bit hypochondriacal are absolutely terrified of cancer. This is probably due to the fact that the general public automatically imagines that if a person has cancer he is as good as dead— or about to die—yet this is far from the truth. I will admit that it is surprising how many people suffer from this disease and how often it is discovered all too late. The truth is that it can be completely painless and so can go unnoticed by the doctor and patient until it reaches an advanced stage.

The very word "cancer" in England is almost taboo, and

it is simply not done to describe the illness of a friend as cancer unless you put your hand to your mouth and whisper it. This is unrealistic, because the disease is very prevalent and, indeed, is one of the most common causes of death—especially in older people. It is said that the incidence of cancer is higher in America than in the United Kingdom. Americans do not hide the extent of the disease, and they have many hospitals devoted entirely to its cure. Their propaganda campaign to educate the general public and local doctors is very highly developed.

Just look at a few statistics. In America, they report that one out of every four who die, dies of cancer. More conservative figures say that it strikes one out of every four people and that vast numbers of these are cured.

In Britain one of the oldest cancer societies, the National Society for Cancer Relief, claims it is one in six, and that more died of cancer during the war years than the total of our war dead and missing.

Cancer hit two out of every three families in America in 1955, and over 235,000 died of cancer—about one every two minutes. In England, people bury their heads in the sands of silence which has bred inertia towards the greatest scourge of mankind, but the Health Report on the nation issued in December 1955 showed a further increase in the number of deaths from cancer. Can we believe statistics? The position is serious, but I would like to see statistics of the many cures.

It is undoubtedly true that cancer is on the increase in the civilized areas of the world. It is natural to ask why this is, and it is suggested by some that either there are more carcinogens in the civilized world or that their high-pressure way of living and eating has something to do with the body imbalance, glandular or chemical, which is cancer's breeding ground. Some regard carcinogens as containing a minute virus which some people can overcome, but this is not proven. It is, of course, true that we know more of the cause of death of millions of people and that this may influence the cancer death-rate figures. It is also true that, now we have cured vast numbers of people of T.B., pneumonia, etc., and prevented the spread of these diseases, we have decreased the number of causes from which people die. Thus the potential number of deaths from cancer or sheer old age is increased.

All of this must not blind us to the fact that it is the major and most complex disease of our generation—a greater killer than any world war so far. Therefore, cancer and its problems must command the serious attention of Christians in order to evolve a "Cancer and Christian Faith" concept. For the ostrich to suggest that it is unimportant and should be treated like any other disease is ridiculous.

Like all diseases, it is of paramount importance that it should be diagnosed as early as possible and this depends on the efficiency of the local doctor, hospital, and the patient's ability to describe his symptoms clearly. I need hardly add that people should be ruthless in seeking a second opinion when in doubt, however much a doctor's feelings may be offended, because a human life is at stake. Doctors may claim that they are never offended, but we lay people often hesitate lest we should be thought hypochondriacs. Under the National Health scheme doctors are busy people, so it is up to the patient to be precise. Their time should not be wasted by chronic malingerers but be directed to those who need them most.

Let me give you a few examples, lest someone should pooh-pooh some complaint of yours. Obviously, a sore that never heals, any unusual bleeding, a swelling in the neck or chest, piles, a mole or birthmark which has become active, need a second opinion, or at least a clinical examination. The thirteen most common places are in the breast, digestive system, lip, mouth, skin, lungs, warts, piles, prostate, throat, tongue, liver, rectum, uterus, and the blood. Usually when it is too late we learn all about a subject, and although physical examination of piles may reveal a cancer, nevertheless additional examinations by instruments and barium enemas are absolutely essential.

A doctor confessed to me the other day that in the last few months he had by instrument examination discovered that seven of his "pile" patients indeed had cancer. Had he not used instruments he would never have known. How few doctors possess a proctoscope. It is quite hopeless to expect a busy general doctor to read all the latest medical treatments of cancer when from morning to night he is filling out forms and preoccupied with childbirth, mumps, measles, and common colds. He hesitates to pronounce cancer and many times does not dare demand priority for his patient from a hospital that is not cancer-conscious. He needs the support of a "Cancer Panel" or "Tumor Clinic" within easy reach, and in turn this centre would pass the patient on to experts according to the site of the cancer. The best cancer detection centre is any *ALERT* doctor's office.

A great deal of the money that we in Britain subscribe to cancer research could go towards improvement of existing facilities of discovering and treating in time this terrible disease. Advice centres leading to cancer-detection clinics and more cancer hospitals are needed. Priority for beds should be given to cancer patients.

I thank God for the generous benefactors who have given to cancer research and given local clinical establishments or equipment. Do not let State medicine rob us of our responsibility to give towards research and reforms. Private enterprise is all too easily replaced by State lethargy unless public opinion is alert.

X rays can go a long way to help in this discovery,

especially with lung cancer; and colon cancer by means of a barium meal in reverse. It must be remembered that X rays are macroscopic and not microscopic.

In other words, they will not show the early stages of any changes in the bone structure in the case of bone disease, for these early stages are microscopic in size, even if they are painful. Needless to say, where there is risk of cancer of the bone, no osteopath should be allowed to do any manipulation. A barium X ray in both directions with the full follow-through is one of the tests for cancer in the digestive tract. In certain hospitals they can now examine these tracts by instruments without performing an exploratory operation if they are not satisfied with the X rays.

Where the X-ray department fails, the pathological laboratory can succeed. A blood test can be taken and this is known as the sedimentation-rate test. This ESR test can sometimes give a fair idea as to whether there is any serious cancer activity going on in the body. This sedimentation-rate test can vary according to the "activity" of the cancer, and so should be repeated to double check if there is reason to doubt. The lower the rate of fall in the first hour in the test tube, the better. This ESR test, if rapid, does not necessarily prove cancer, but sounds the alarm that something is wrong.

The New Smear Test. Various other tests are being developed and in America, where they have many cancer-detection clinics, they have the painless Papanicolaou vaginal-smear test by which cancer cells may be detected as much as eight to ten years before they become dangerous. It is claimed for this test that it has saved the lives of thousands of women. This test is sometimes disappointing with its false negatives in lung or vaginal smears. We all hope that one day a simple blood test will be evolved, which will prove the existence of cancer long before it breaks out into obvious manifestations. But as yet this is a

dream, because they have not found a common denom-
inator amongst the many and complex forms which come
under the heading of cancer.

The pathologists with the latest type of powerful microscope can diagnose cancer, once the slide with its tiny piece
of tissue from a suspicious tumor is in position.

This test involves an operation called a biopsy, which
varies in degree according to the position of the suspicious
growth. A sample piece is cut off and sent to the pathological laboratory while the surgeon waits in the operating
theatre for the verdict. The sample is frozen and then cut
flat so that it can be placed on a convenient slide under the
microscope. In a matter of seconds the pathologist pro-
nounces his verdict and the surgeon either closes up the
wound or proceeds to a radical operation. He takes care to
remove the primary growth as well as the channels and
the focal points where the cancer metastases may have
travelled.

I have heard it said that every seven years there is a cell
change in the human body—but it does not necessarily follow that cancer comes in the wake of such a change.

The late Lord Horder, one of Britain's leading physi-
cians, has said: "Cancer is such a common disease after the
age of forty years that in examining every patient past this
age *cancer must always be in the doctor's mind*. The onus
at once becomes this—to prove that the lesion is *not* cancerous. A spirit of unrest must activate the doctor's mind
until he has eliminated the possibility of early malignant
disease. In many cases there is a reasonable margin of time
between the local and potentially curable stage of cancer
and the generalized and incurable stage. It is this margin
which offers a fertile field for the doctor's skill. The reward
for such skill may be the saving of the life of a fellow
human being." Since Lord Horder's day they say that at
any age the onus is to disprove cancer.

Again the question arises: "What is cancer?" Science is on the very brink of discovery, but to put down the cause to worry, overwork and smoking—or even to God Himself—is not the answer. Worry does indeed weaken the resistance of the body to any germ invasion, and some people are the worrying kind when it comes to matters of business and money. It is so easy for someone to tell you that worry is a want of faith and that you must trust God, but maybe they do not realize what a heavy load of responsibility bears down on some people. The thick-skinned and the happy-go-lucky find it easy to off-load their worries on to God, or on to other people. Or they just trust to luck. There are millions of sensitive creatures who, like a violin, are vibrant to the heavy responsibilities they have to bear. Some of these responsibilities cannot be just palmed off on to God in a *laissez-faire* manner. They have to be worked out logically with God.

It is all too easy to blame duodenal ulcers, cancer, and everything else on worry. A very high percentage of men are potential ulcer cases and cancer cases—more so than women, with the one exception of cancer of the breast. The male is the more delicate of the species. These, we are told, are people who live on their nerves: taxi drivers, politicians, and high-powered businessmen. Indeed, it is generally accepted to be true that overworry does far more harm to the human body than any amount of overwork. Matrimonial unhappiness is a common cause of ulcers. Some doctors firmly believe that worry causes the glands at the base of the skull to discharge a wrong balance of hormones, thus upsetting the chemical balance of the body and creating the state for cancer to develop. If this be a basic underlying factor, how important it is for a "cure" that we learn more about Christian faith healing and adjust ourselves to composed gracious living! I have a new set of non-medical hormones which I call the hormones of faith, courage, sheer grit and humour. I think they are very powerful if only you can release them. They are certainly handmaidens of the doctor and this is where the padre comes in.

The scientists have warned us that there seems to be a close relationship between smoking and cancer of the lungs. The Horn-Hammond report states that the lung-cancer death rate is three times greater for heavy cigarette smokers. It says that the disease is rare among non-smokers. If, indeed, heavy smoking causes an increase of the incidence of cancer, this should shake a far greater number of chain smokers out of this carcinogenic habit.

"Oh, it cannot happen to me," says the chain smoker who is either living in a fool's paradise or not enjoying life enough to want to live long.

I know there is, fortunately, a tendency for all of us never to believe that the worst can happen to us. This is a natural protective crust with which we surround ourselves and it keeps us from being morbid and unadventurous in the face of a very tough world.

I remember the same feeling just before we crashed in an air liner at Gander in 1946, after crossing the Atlantic on two out of four engines. I remember watching, in a calm and fascinated manner, the tops of the pine trees flashing by as we lost height approaching Newfoundland. When the crash came, and one had recovered from what felt like a blow at the back of the neck, the reaction was to say to oneself in surprise: "Heavens, it's us . . . it's happened to us . . . where's the door . . . we must get out of here before it catches fire."

When the crash of cancer comes, it is too late to stop chain smoking.

It is said there is something in Diesel-oil fumes which is known to be a carcinogen—a cancer-producing agent—for lung cancer. There is an alarming increase in the incidence of this disease in cities as against the country. The facts are undeniable. One research laboratory has listed two hundred carcinogens including many chemicals used in industry, some of which have been withdrawn. Cancer of the bladder can come from certain chemicals used among dye, rubber and plastic workers, cancer of the skin can come to fingers of tar workers and of older radiologists, cancer of the bone to men working with luminous paint, and so forth.

You may well ask: "What is cancer?"

The human body is made up of cells which grow in the allotted way and size. Cancer cells have neither nerves nor blood, yet grow in an untidy, uncontrolled manner. They are parasites and draw nourishment from their hosts, like ivy. The cancer cell has an inner cell and within this is a line called a chromosome. This chromosome has bumps on the top and bottom of it. Some say the under bump towards the right controls the rate of growth or germination. Others express it thus . . . that in good cells the nucleoproteins determine the characteristics of new subdividing cells which normally become good members of the body, doing their allotted job of work. But that if, through an imbalance of body, the "carcinogenic virus" succeeds in attacking the nucleoproteins, the cells then created have changed characters, i.e., cancer. These do not co-operate with the rest of the body, but think of nothing but growing and are greedy for oxygen. Many regard the root of the trouble to be a virus of either the active or dormant kind, and that this can be brought to life in an imbalanced body either by an unknown factor or by stress-produced white blood cells or by the direct application of a carcinogenic substance or radiation which gives life to the virus which then changes the character of the nucleoprotein, so that cancer cells result. They think that the basic secret will be found in the imbalance of the intercellular fluids stemming from the pituitary gland. It is interesting to note that stress uses up white cells in the blood and that the replacement cells known by some scientists as "stress-produced white blood cells" are somewhat different to normal white cells. I find the reports in this field intensely interesting. The basis of the cure or arresting action is the "attack" on the lower growth bump of the chromosome right inside the cancer cell or on the nucleoproteins around the affected area.

This attack is carried out by radium, thanks to Marie Curie, by radium implants, cobalt 60, by new artificially produced isotopes and by chemical nitrogen mustard. This kills the cell and the oxygen supply, but does not correct any imbalance of the general body. The last two forces have proved very successful indeed in Britain and so we are on the brink of discoveries which may quickly change the whole field of cancer suffering. In association with the above, there is a widely held theory that a chemical cellular imbalance of the body sometimes arises owing to some disturbance of the glands, and this situation forms the breeding ground for the invasion of cancer. Some say, therefore, that we must put right the balance of the glands and the intercellular fluid, and that then the cancer will disappear. At the present stage of knowledge we must cut out the outward and visible signs of cancer—namely, the growth. Palliative effect is gained by removing certain glands such as the adrenal or by administering hormones.

Carcinomas, as these growths are called, are in themselves completely painless, and left to themselves they multiply quite quickly. Alternatively they may be very slow in growing and multiplying and may take years building up. Carcinoma of the breast often shows itself as a lump just below the actual nipple, long before it hurts. The question obviously arises as to when it does start hurting. When the cancer cells fasten themselves on to a nerve or a muscle which naturally contains nerves, or any other vital organ—then the pain is excruciating indeed. Added to this is the nuisance—or "physical worry-value"—of a growth in some part of the body to the annoyance and irritation of the rest of the organs. This can cause bleeding and the cancer itself can bleed. This is the paramount sign which really sounds the alarm.

Cancer of the intestines, apart from periods of extreme colic or pain, worries the whole peristaltic movement to such a degree that it causes a backwash of indigestion which can be mistaken for a return of duodenal-ulcer trouble. I would sometimes complain that it felt as if the peristaltic movement had gone into reverse. At other times, it was as if the whole pelvis was aching, and at the centre was something gnawing and drawing you down. If I could have pushed sticks of ice inside, I would cheerfully have done so, for it was burning hot and often bleeding.

The first appearance of cancer is the "primary" growth, or to us lay people a "first incident," and it is very rare to get two utterly separate, unconnected primaries. Cancer cells may travel along the blood stream, through muscles or nerves and very frequently along the "lymphatics" or, in other words, fluid ducts or channels which resemble a rosary. A rosary has a sort of chain of small beads, and then at regular intervals are large beads. The large beads in the lymphatics are called nodes. From the primary attack of cancer, it spreads down these lymphatics to the next port of call.

When an operation is performed, it is most important not merely to remove the primary growth, but to remove as many of the surrounding lymphatics as possible. In my case, I had the benefit of a "ruthless" surgeon who removed two inches more of each lymphatic beyond the visible tumor than later laboratory tests showed was necessary, as well as all the rectum, sigmoid colon, and part of the pelvic walls. He was taking no chances of missing an evil

cell, in order to reduce as far as possible the chances of a
secondary starting up. He removed what amounted to
dozens of yards of lymphatic channels.

A secondary is when cancer has travelled along a lymphatic or other route and settled down somewhere else.
This requires a second operation or deep X ray to destroy
it. It is the secondary which all of us cancer patients fear,
and unfortunately you cannot be sure that the cancer has
gone for good till five years have elapsed after the primary
operation.

Today some surgeons in America are adopting the practice of taking a "second look," or even more looks, about
six months after the first operation. In Minnesota, out of
fifty-three colon cancer second looks, about fifteen had to
have further bits of cancer removed.

With cancer of the breast, they not only remove the
whole breast but the lymphatics and nodes from breast to
armpit—right round under the breast and back to the arm.
Taken in time and with this extensive surgery, they elimi-
nate as far as is humanly possible the chance of a secondary. I know of a case of a woman who had hers done
twenty-five years ago, and she is still an excellent secretary.
She had little pain before the operation, and once a few
months had gone by she was free of pain.

In contrast, I know of a very tragic case of a man whose
little ulcer in the mouth proved to be cancer. They removed
the cancer ulcer and killed the surrounding lymphatics
with deep X ray. Eighteen months later he reported at
another hospital for breathlessness and was X-rayed. There
in the right lung was a carcinoma as large as a grapefruit.
The first X rays were sent for, and there on the plate was
the same carcinoma as large as a walnut. Somebody had
not noticed it! (Most specialists insist on seeing the plates
for themselves.) Two primaries in one person! He could
not be operated on for two weeks, and the night before the

operation he died of a rapid secondary striking the liver. His brother, a doctor, deeply regrets the mistake.

For years they have been treating cancer with radium and deep X ray, and the idea is to destroy the cancer. This may be necessary to arrest various cancers, but while it is not painful at the time, it may be afterwards. It requires great skill and painstaking mathematics to hit the right spot for the right length of time. Imagine deciding and then directing two rays into the body from different positions; the point inside where they cross is the spot to be treated. It is not necessarily a cure, but can slow up the situation. Ray treatment on cancer of the skin can completely clear it up. Early skin cancer is usually not very painful, but eventually becomes a sore which will not heal.

Great hopes lie in the use of isotopes, a product of atomic energy, to attack the growth, particularly in the lung. Once they really can, through atomic rays or through chemistry, create cancer, they may learn how to kill it. But can they ever trace its cause before it starts? Some say it is caused through a wrong chemical balance of food—others blame out-of-balance discharges of hormones from two glands at the base of the brain which, in turn, may be controlled through worry and stress. In the Sloan-Kettering research laboratory, which is linked with two research wards in the Memorial Hospital, New York, Dr. Toolan has succeeded in growing in test tubes human cancer taken from a patient. When this was implanted on the arms of fourteen volunteers in an Ohio prison, it would not "take" and soon "fell off." Some chemical balance in their bodies was not allergic to cancer. But when the cancer was returned, by agreement, to the original owner it immediately thrived as it did with other cancer patients. If all of this is authenticated, it may point to the importance of the constitution of the individual. These two wards specialise in experiments for metabolic and chemotherapy with courageous human volunteers who know that they are terminal cases.

It has been established that there are certain carcinogens, oil, soot, dirt, etc. Many famous cancer specialists have no doubt in their minds about the link between cigarette smoking and lung cancer. Dr. William Bond of Birmingham, England, says that:

"In our cities the concentration of cancer-producing agents in the air is sometimes equivalent to someone smoking two hundred cigarettes a day, even to the non-smoker. Cigarette smoke contains the same cancer-producing agent as city air but in greater concentration and the cigarette-smoker is thus in a trebly vulnerable position."

Anyone who knows anything of the seriousness of cancer in the lungs would be wise to take this warning very much to heart.

A very interesting new development in England is H.11 Therapy when applied to cancer of the lung. Since cancer of the lung accounts for fifteen thousand deaths a year in England and Wales, anything which can help in this field commands great attention. So far, H.11 has only been applied to the so-called "hopeless" cases after the 30 per cent of hopefuls have been selected for surgery or deep X ray. It is claimed that for these remaining tough cases, often being applied very late, H.11 benefits them in that their expectation of life is prolonged—doubled—and during this extended life many of them live free of pain with an improvement in their general outlook. Thus it relieves suffering and eases the manner of their dying. H.11 acts slowly in the blood stream and the results take time to show themselves. These who believe in it would like to see it applied early and not just at the very last moment, to the most difficult cases.

Opponents of H.11 claim that they have tested it and found it to be useless, but many doctors write in saying how helpful they find it. Somewhat similar claims have been made in America for different serums. Medical opinion is divided on many new drugs or serums, and this is to be expected even when they emanate from qualified doctors at the research level.

The problem is, indeed, so complex that new drugs and serums will come and go till the medical profession finds the answer to the problem, and it may not be one answer, for cancer takes so many forms. We should always be on our guard against quacks who will exploit a so-called new cure, either for the sake of money or because they have a genuine consuming desire to help, and are apt to reduce the problem to a simple unscientific level.

Now I want to reassure any reader that there are certain cures and slowing-up processes for cancer, and that to have the disease does not mean certain death. There are many who would call across the world to you if they knew you by name, and bear testimony that they had been cured and were still going strong, either as a result of modern surgery, medical treatment, or divine healing. In all of these cases, the personal determination of the patient—the will to win—is vital to the doctors and to God and ofttimes, I am sure, it is combinations of all three. We hear so little of the successful cures that people find it difficult to believe there are any. People do not believe a doctor's reassurances, because they know only of the cases who have died. They have factual evidence for this, and if they knew more of the technical names for cancer on thousands and thousands of death certificates, they would believe doctors even less.

Something has got to be done about this, and here, I believe, my concept "Cancer Anonymous" will be able to help. The doctor is bound by secrecy and, much as he would like to, he cannot list the names of the victorious cancer cases, so the dark cloud of doubt and fatalistic fear deepens. People begin to imagine that the silence indicates that there are no permanent cures worth talking about.

Modern surgery is the result of man's development of the God-given gift of medical science, and it can eradicate the disease in one operation, provided not a single malignant cell is left behind. If they do miss one, they have to chase the disease all over the body, as it spreads its crablike tentacles into either muscle tissue or bone structure or some vital organ. In this way they can prolong life for the patient or cure this disease completely. Cancer of the throat, mouth, or lip can be cured, chiefly by radio therapy. Cancer of the lungs is not the easiest place for it to develop from the point of view of a cure.

Modern research by people like Dr. Fleming has resulted in the discovery of penicillin, which saves millions of lives and prevents painful septic wounds, and they have discovered something which will attack certain of the virus diseases such as polio. Pathologists are working unceasingly to discover an injection which will attack and win the battle over cancer.

It has been found that some animals and possibly some humans are more susceptible to cancer than others, and scientists are endeavouring to discover the reason for this. They will go on to the stage of correcting the mechanisms of the likely cases so that they can build up enough "antibodies" to kill off the cancer cells.

Antiserums have been tried out with a measure of success on animals by such people as Dr. John Graham of Boston, Dr. J. J. Bittner of London, Ontario, Dr. Bertil Bjorklund of Stockholm, and Dr. R. W. Wissler of Chicago.

In the field of radiation, the experiments with radioactive cobalt have helped to melt away cancer in the lung and liver. Cobalt 60 is artificially radioactivated cobalt in the atomic pile, a product of atomic research. A 1500-curie cobalt unit emits highly penetrating radiations of almost a single wave length. Assuming that we had enough radium to take its place, it would cost millions of dollars instead of a few thousand. The characteristics of cobalt 60 may prove to be an important turning point in modern radiotherapy; but cobalt 60 is no panacea and cannot be expected to cure radio-resistant cancer. Improvement of results are expected in cancer of the cervix, bladder, larynx, etc. Between 40 and 45 per cent of *all* women with cancer of the cervix, in all stages of the disease, are cured by adequate irradiation. This may mean weeks of daily but painless treatment. Radioactive iodine has helped to save the lives of children with cancer of the thyroid. Another by-product of the atom bomb—namely, tiny radioactive beads of yttrium oxide have been used to destroy the pituitary gland at the base of the brain. The British are making great strides in the field of radiation and drugs. In the field of drugs there are the following: Purinethol for leukemia (cancer of the blood), TEM for ovarian cancer, and Myleran, Aminopterin and Puromycin. Meanwhile, surgical operations are an endeavour to stem the tide and bring relief to thousands. I am one of those who hope to live on a long time as a result of this—thanks to a ruthless surgeon.

I will deal with the patient's part in all this in the next chapter, but this chapter would not be complete without some reference to divine healing. I cannot say that I have experienced it for myself. I am determined to explore this field and find out as much about it as I can.

I would like to see united services of prayer, thanksgiving and healing taking place in the most impressive manner in fine beautiful churches for cancer patients and ex-patients. Here, in a corporate act of public worship, they can lay down their problems and fears before the throne of God. The tenor of the services must radiate an air of expectancy.

Let us remember that at this present stage of medical knowledge we still have to remove the outward and visible growth and treat the disease with the maximum of medical skill. But it does not need much intelligence to realise the power of the mind and spirit over the pituitary gland, which is like the orchestra conductor presiding over the whole symphony of the human body.

It has so often been found that cancer cells appear in a person following in the wake of great mental stress, worry, and matrimonial unhappiness. This creates two things—first a new type of replacement white cells in the blood stream, and secondly an imbalance of the pituitary which in turn creates an imbalance of the intercellular fluids. This imbalance creates the very condition in which the character forming element (nucleoproteins,) of the cells can be altered by either a cancer virus or carcinogenic agent or both.

It does not require much stretch of imagination to work backwards and presuppose that "spontaneous regression" could come from the correcting of the balance to the pituitary. But how? If worry could disturb it, surely peace of mind, faith in God, act of determination, wanting to get well, a catastrophic miracle of God, could set it right? Then, when the mind and will, through a conscious act of faith and the continuance of the same, has set right the pituitary, cancer regression (healing), may follow.

Now not everyone is healed by this combined "self-and-God" faith process, but that does not disprove divine healing or the power of the mind. Standard medical treatment often fails, and yet often succeeds where there is active "patient co-operation" and faith in God. Ask any doctor what he thinks of the necessity of the patient's urge to get well.

This urge is a crisis affair as well as a long-term policy. I believe in the crisis of conversion—a moment of decision

—followed by a process. Obviously this does not work for all, and indeed some are repelled by the evangelist who seeks to shake you out of a rut. But there is no getting away from it—it does work for many, despite the backsliders. Likewise I think "a crisis followed by a process" cure could come through a public healing service through an inward and outward act of faith through the laying on of hands, at the altar rail with the co-operation of many praying witnesses. Jesus generated, by his presence and reputation before a crowd of expectant witnesses, the atmosphere ingredients for a "patient and God" healing or cure. It needs no stretch of belief or credulity at all to understand that group of His miracles which were a conquest or readjustment of mind and pituitary over matter. Let us start at a point where we can walk with God before we start to run, whilst we go hand in hand with doctors who have developed the skill that God gave them. So we tread into the field of co-operation between the medical profession and the Church. I would like to see more healing services along these lines, and I am sure God would use them to inject the spiritual "shock" to an expectant, longing to keep well, postoperative ex-cancer patient. Few of us priests know if God could use healing in our hands, and we hesitate because we know how utterly unworthy we are.

When we have taken away such elements as wrong diagnosis, fakes and recurrences, there still is a residual quantity of healed cases which command our attention.

You can read of people being cured of cancer by divine or faith healing. Don't let this thought shock you into a general unbelief of many of the things that I have been trying to tell you. God does work in a very mysterious way. There are more things than faith healing that are inexplicable, so let us consider one or two aspects of this. We dare not rule out the miraculous entirely, and to my mind, surgery coupled with human resilience is a form of miracle.

Jesus performed miracles and healed a great number of people. He did not go into detail as to why these people were sick, nor did He explain why He did not heal many, many thousands more. The fact remains that He did perform a number of miracles of healing which go beyond the category of merely mind over matter.

In other words, He did not just heal people who had nothing organically wrong, He healed people who were definitely ill, like the man with the withered arm, and even the dead, like Lazarus, and many other cases.

The healings were, for the most part, associated with two things: firstly He usually touched them, and secondly, He demanded faith in them. You have either got to tell yourself that these are fables, and in fact all miracles are fables, even the miracle of the Incarnation and the Resurrection, or you accept one of them. Then, if you accept one, why not more than one? It is no solution merely to accept the kind of miracles which could be explained away. Yes, He definitely did perform miracles which were inexplicable and which brought cures to people who had physical complaints and not merely mental illness.

We know that the mind plays a great part in illness and there are many pains which will disappear once the root of the trouble in the mind is overcome. Part of the Christian teaching down the ages is the science of the healing of the mind and spirit through personal conversion to a personal Christ. This is in itself a miracle, for it really is the birth of Christ in an individual's heart.

Christian "Faith" is God working in our souls for true conversion, and is something new and of God which we allow to grow up from within us.

This new birth which was so clearly explained to Nicodemus in the third chapter of St. John is the very basis of Christianity, and, rightly grasped, heals a great deal of the woes of man and is a new medicine for living. William

James in his book, *The Variety of Religious Experiences*, analyses the evidences of conversion and admits that this miracle of a changed personality does take place like a medical case history.

The elements in it are the spiritual touch of God and the individual's faith to absorb God. If you doubt this "new birth" miracle, I can only suggest that you examine the evidence of many witnesses or seek out such a Christian for yourself and study him. The Roman Catholic Church has many healing shrines which cannot be ignored.

These are indeed matters of the soul, and millions never experience these things, but live their span in this world without any rhyme or reason. In them is not found any burning desire to serve or work for the enlightenment and betterment of their fellow men. They live dull, self-centred, colourless lives, chained to the prison of materialism from which beauty, colour, music and scenery can only lift them for a moment to rattle their chains.

The mystery certainly is still unanswered as to why Christ only healed a limited number and why His early disciples healed far less and why this gift seems to have lapsed. The gift of healing has not entirely lapsed, for at resurgent moments in the last two thousand years it has undeniably reappeared.

Some explain that the definite gift of healing was "permitted" by God in the early days for the founding and creation of Christendom. It was "allowed" to lapse, but God brought the treasure of the renaissance in the wake of Christianity. This knowledge has reached a very high degree, yet we constantly hear of cases of a short circuit through divine healing.

There are men and women alive today to whom God has entrusted the gift of healing in their hands. Some say it is the fault of Christians down the ages for having ignored this extraordinary gift, but at least, today, it is receiving recognition.

While there may be quacks who deceive in the very name of Christ in order to make money, there are evidences of devout men and women through whom God can heal. They usually anoint with oil or cup the hands in prayer and then pray over the patient and lay their hands on him.

I recommend you as well as myself to seek out these people and ask their help and how we can help them. Although I cannot explain why God uses them as an agent, I am convinced that a cure can come this way. It is a mystery why one man has the power of a healer and why one patient is cured and not another.

We cannot explain how divine healing occurs through the laying on of hands. We cannot explain much of this world, nor suffering itself, but we just have to accept it, so let's accept divine healing in whatever form. But watch out for fakers who are only out for money even though they deny it.

Here is what is said on this subject by James in Chapter 5, verses 14–16:

Is any sick among you? Let him call for the elders of the church; and let them pray over him, anointing him with oil in the name of the Lord:

And the prayer of faith shall save the sick, and the Lord shall raise him up; and if he have committed sins, they shall be forgiven him.

Confess your faults one to another, and pray one for another, that ye may be healed. The effectual fervent prayer of a righteous man availeth much.

God today heals through doctors and surgeons, and through priests and laity with definite gifts of healing. Sometimes through His Divine Touch there comes a complete mental healing and deliverance from fear and worry, though I do not think that freedom from fear occurs on one occasion and operates for all time, but there can be moments of victorious crisis. Freedom from fear and worry is a daily battle, more bitter for some than for others. It means convinced living in the power of God. It would seem that it puts right the balance of the glands, so do not be unbelieving.

In spiritual healing, people are brought nearer to God and to His will in their lives through the extraordinary Divine Touch or by the anointing of holy oil.

There is evidence that complete physical healing can be brought to a person in this way. It is still one of the mysteries that some people seem to be called upon to go through what can only be described as "redemptive suffering." Suffering, pain, and evil definitely exist, and to believe otherwise is neither scientific nor Christian.

With God's guidance, seek out your idea of a man of God among the truly dedicated priests of God and pour out your soul to him.

I hope to evolve trained priests, who possess an unshakable faith in Christ, and who will understand the cancer problem as it affects patients and relatives and I call them CANCER ANONYMOUS COUNSELLORS. They will not be doctors, but they will at least be able to break the bread of God to you.

They may be God's instrument of healing to you in more ways than one: there will be a big fee for divine healing— the gift of your whole self and your substance in gratitude to the work of Christ's kingdom. You will need to live a calm dedicated life in service of God's creatures. I have read of cases in which proven cancer has been cured through the laying on of hands both in private and in a public service. Yes, it is a mystery. The "cupping of the hands," the consecrated oil, and the laying on of hands are the focal points of concentrated faith.

You must have this burning desire to live and to wrest this victory from God for yourself, using His "gifted channels."

Just to help your faith in the unknown mysteries of the resurgence of the human body, let me tell you that every once in a while scientists know that human beings do spontaneously recover from cancer.

It is evident that suddenly something in their bodies controls the malignancy or cancer growth and beats it out of existence. It is called spontaneous regression, and who knows how or why this ever comes about?

Now we have yet to find out what causes cancer (carcinogens), and conversely, what sometimes causes cancer to disappear. What scientists are trying to find out is what chemical in the body causes this favourable "antibody" reaction which attacks and wins the battle over the cancer cells. This "antibody" formation is to me a really hopeful line of thought, for all discoveries in the long run prove to be basically simple. If only we could discover how patients could create their own anticancer material, then the knowledge could at least be used on the less advanced cases of cancer.

A proper balance of hormones, maybe? So the idea of God adjusting the balance in a person by faith healing is not such a remote cure after all, even to the sceptical. Cannot the pulsating faith and determination of the human brain set forth discharges of chemical reaction as an antibody? Can some new drug one day soon stimulate that discharge?

Rest assured that in every country enormous efforts in the field of research are being made and very great strides have been made to combat this most ghastly disease experienced by man. Scientists and the more knowledgeable doctors know a great deal about it, despite the fact that it originates from within the body and is not "caught" from somebody else. Although in its early stages it is not necessarily painful, it can be "spotted" (diagnosed) by the skilful doctor with the aid of modern equipment, almost wherever it appears. To my way of thinking, we in Britain have not enough research going on where the problem of human cancer is concerned. In fact there must be a revolution or break through soon . . . away from basic research to clinical research.

It can be "cured" or "eradicated" or "stemmed" by qualified medical practitioners, *especially* if caught in time. Thus it is absolutely vital, if we are to reduce the alarming tide of death and suffering, that people should not be afraid to report the earliest possible signs to their doctor, even at the risk of being accused of having a cancer phobia.

As to the outbreak of "secondaries," we can take courage that a good hospital in co-operation with the local doctor is on the lookout over patients, and they know what signs to expect according to the original primary.

Colon cancer and breast cancer, once operated upon in sufficient time, have the best prognosis. I have lived through two years without a secondary striking my liver, and I shall be glad when the five-year period is up so that I can join the ranks of those who live to a ripe old age. I know of one cancer case who lived with a colostomy for over forty years and died at one hundred and six years of age.

There are many forms of cancer far more terrible and more difficult than mine, but for them as well as for all in pain, it is vital to keep alive within ourselves a personal determination. The fighting spirit and the faith of each individual sufferer, bolstered up by a lively trust in God, can work wonders.

I venture to prophesy that the lasting cure for cancer will be found in the field of the chemistry of the human body and cell metabolism. Once this secret is discovered, a chemotherapy treatment will arise which will go to the very root of the disease and will one day replace the surgeon's knife and the scientist's rays.

CHAPTER 16

Cancer Anonymous

LITTLE did I know when I began this book in that Los Angeles hospital with a tape recorder that it was going to take so long to finish and mean so much to me. It began with the idea of helping a few people, actually in hospital with cancer, by means of a very small booklet. But as life went on and each week brought fresh commitments and a deepening experience, I have begun to realize the immense toll of human suffering.

I am so grateful to be alive that I am in agony of mind to know what I can do to help others as a means of expressing my gratitude both to God and to my fellow men. The greatest need, as I see it, is to stimulate faith, hope, and morale as the vital elements in the battle, for we must never give in to cancer.

I have asked God for time to wear His shoes—the prodigal son's shoes—and I know full well that the "converted pagan" has a responsibility to those still living in the far country. A new Christian must not merely sit down peacefully in the company of his new-found Christian friends and enjoy the sweet fruits of a new way of life. He must go back to the far country where sin and suffering abound, making sure that his feet are shod with the preparation of the Gospel of Christ. He must be an "Identified Christian" in that far country.

I have the shoes of a new life with new experience which must be shared with those whose souls are twisted and tortured as a result of the physical excruciating pain of cancer. I must share the news of victory over this dread disease with those who fear it, lest they should continue to imagine that cancer means death every time. I must help to give others the will to live and the courage to hang on to God. I must help to relieve their suffering with the milk of human kindness.

This dark and foul skeleton which thrives on secrecy and hides in the furtive imagination of the average person, causing fear, depression, and a conviction of certain defeat, must be brought out of the cupboard and seen for what it is worth.

The Egyptians in the dim past dreaded it, and down the ages man has striven to defeat it. Men dreaded it so much they thought it was unclean, contagious, hereditary, and inevitable. Therefore, we have still with us today the conspiracy of silence concerning it which only goes to increase the suffering it causes by haunting the minds of the healthy, as well as of the afflicted and their relatives.

Along with this conspiracy of secrecy has gone the ominous knowledge that the death rate is more heavy every year, despite all the efforts of surgeons and the advent of radioactive substances. Who does not know someone in the family circle whose death was due to cancer? It is utterly futile to wave away the fearful by sneeringly accusing them of being hypochondriacs. How impervious to their worry-caused suffering to withhold all information on the subject of cancer because the general public are thought to be so imbecile that they cannot be trusted with medical information lest they subside into utter despondency! Instead they subside into ignorance, which breeds fear, which is increased by the knowledge that 280 known deaths are occurring every day in Britain from cancer.

What is there to hide? Could it be that there are no
cures worth speaking of? Is it that it is useless to raise
people's hopes for a cure even after all these years of research and activity? Can hope and optimism help the
public and the patient alike and be built on a sure foundation? Yes, there are grounds for hope—there are many cures
—it can be endured, so do not give up the battle for life.

Five years after treatment the survival rate without re-
currence, in certain forms of cancer, is as follows:

FOR CANCER OF:	TREATED EARLY	MODERATELY ADVANCED	TREATED LATE
Skin	95%	60%	20%
Cervix Uteri	65% to 90%	35%	5%
Mouth and lip	64%	25%	5%
Breast	55% to 85%	30%	4%
Throat	53%	15%	3%

In America they say that 45 per cent of *all* women with
cancer of the cervix, in all stages, are cured by adequate
irradiation. This may mean weeks of painless treatment.

I consider that it is absolutely vital that we should raise
the confident hope and knowledge concerning the cures
and treatment for cancer in the mind of the general public,
and this will enable doctors to take patients and relatives
more into their confidence concerning the illness of a patient. Then all, by their very attitude, will radiate confidence, hope, and courage, and this will reflect on the
patient.

At the present time too many people consciously and
unconsciously radiate defeat, and surround their sick relatives with the worst possible atmosphere, instead of ra-
diating optimism. Some people are so ignorant that they
imagine there is something shameful about cancer. They
falsely imagine it is a disease that is dirty; they falsely imagine that it's catching and hereditary. They burn the bed-

ding when people die. Ludicrous behaviour built on a tissue of lies, framed by this awful barrier of silence and ignorance of victory. Small wonder the poor devil who gets cancer suddenly finds himself surrounded by people who behave in this way. If the poor man has never been told previously of the successful cure of patients, he will automatically believe he is as good as dead if he suspects cancer.

This silence breeds lies. Doctors and relatives lie to a patient and pretend that he has got anything else but cancer. Nine times out of ten the poor wretched man guesses it and starts lying back to his relatives lest he should upset them, in a kind of merry-go-round, which the professional social worker pretends is helpful all around. In truth, some social workers and clergy are cowards or simply do not understand the mentality of a great many cancer patients. If patients guess the truth and at the same time haven't the slightest idea that it has ever been cured, what living hell they go through! They can't even have an honest talk with their doctor. At least relatives can talk openly to their doctor and get optimistic news, but the patient is often treated as an imbecile to whom we must tell a tissue of lies. His life is at stake. Surely, in many cases, he has a right to know so he can summon his body to beat it. But he must know of victory first. I only hope that somewhere, somehow, in the years before, when they were quite well, they either read this book or heard the theme of Cancer Anonymous bringing the news to them that *cancer can be cured or endured,* and bringing the one and only basis for the spirit of man, namely, personal living individual faith in God. No surgeon worth his salt will deny the healing powers of human endeavour and faith in God. So the most sick patient can read this book. Maybe you are reading it now as a result of a gift from a friend who only desires to help you as I do.

One of the most vexed questions in the medical world,

both from surgeons, matrons and others, is this question of
whether we should tell the patient. In England, by and
large, they do not tell the patient. In fact they tell them
direct lies, saying that it is an ulcer, etc. Some claim that
they do not tell direct lies, but they leave it to the poor
Ward Sister to do the direct lying. The net result is this
thoroughly unhealthy attitude that exists in Great Britain
on this subject. It is not so much apathy about cancer, it is
positive fear, because nobody has the courage to tell the
nation of the positive side. It makes me sick when I listen
to some adolescent doctor hiding behind "Of course you
know, you must not raise false hopes."

Whilst you cannot generalise, and say that you must tell
every patient, or on the other hand that you must never
tell a patient, I consider that far more people should be
told than are being told at present, especially if you have
grounds to suspect that they already know, or are likely to
find out. Of course, if the patient is already an imbecile,
then go on treating him like an imbecile, but if he has got
any intelligence, and certainly any faith, his co-operation
inwardly with the treatment, will be of infinite value to the
surgeon, radiotherapist or doctor.

This confidence is vital to the doctor, and truth plays a
part in it. Doctors are constantly faced with the problem of
what to tell a patient and when to withhold information. It
is a very difficult question, and I would like to mention a
number of aspects to be considered. If a doctor honestly
believes that the truth about a nervous patient's serious illness would do him harm, he has to balance this against the
risk of the patient finding out down the road, from another
doctor or from a nurse or from the high level of public
medical information in popular magazines. When the patient finds he has been deceived by his favourite doctor
no amount of plausible explanation will suffice or restore
healing confidence in that doctor.

However much of a healing personality the doctor may have, the damage of mutual trust has been done. Even if the doctor claims he has not told a direct lie, he may have involved the wife or husband in what must become a cascade of lies.

The patient so often relies on the beloved wife or husband to find out the truth from the doctor and tell the truth, and when he finds that even she has been lying to him as well, then utter despair and disillusionment sets in, and he can become utterly disgusted. He may cease to believe anyone again about anything, least of all his health or prognosis, even though it may honestly have turned a corner for good. He is alone in his bed, and there is nothing else but to roll up and die. His love, marriage and sacred trust may seem to him a dastardly shambles—all in a good cause, no doubt. This is now the cancer of the mind and the chaplain is possibly the only person who can get "near" him now.

Many patients have told me, as a priest, that they "know" and that they die with the bond of loyalty with their husband soiled by lies. I hope never to be sent to the grave in this way . . . I would want to take the load off my wife and face it together and enjoy complete understanding right to the end. To restore breaches made by deceit may take longer than life has to offer. We can clear the patients' minds of wrong ideas, and they can help towards their own healing.

I think most potentially terminal cases have a right to know in order to die at peace with their Maker, or to have some time to put their affairs in order to protect their dependents, for so many forget to make a will. They may also, by their effort, beat death by the miracle of determination. Of course, it is obvious that it must not just be one doctor's opinion, because a fresh mind to the situation may save a life. Doctors differ very much, and, if self-opinionated, resent a second opinion, or a new line of treatment. This is a very real problem, and a frequent human problem.

I claim that with cancer more than any other disease, the patient or his family has a right to a second opinion on the treatment, especially if the patient is going downhill, or in the face of a terminal prognosis by *one* doctor. They should be told about this even if they do not ask, for a life is at stake where metastasis has started.

Whoever heard of a court of law sentencing a man to death without informing the prisoner or giving the defence council the right of a fair trial and the right of appeal? Whoever heard of a court of law leaving a man in prison without trial till he died waiting? Whoever puts a man, known to have a tumor, on a hospital waiting list for six months or two years, for a bed? YES, IT HAS BEEN DONE, and has been found out.

I would be dead now if I had not fought for my own life, so I thank God again and again for the man who told me he could not operate, and that I would die in three or four days. He gave me the chance to find another answer. My wife might have just waited for my death, not daring to tell me.

There is a legal aspect of the problem when a patient is deceived to the point of death, and thus the patient is deprived of the opportunity to fight or get a second opinion. Time and again doctors are proved wrong, and a new doctor with a fresh approach or more experience may succeed. Anyway, cancer foxes all of us, because so often the worst cases live on and on when they should be dead.

There are a number of classic true stories—the woman who had leukemia for thirty years and refused to die; the elderly lady whose chief occupation for the last five years was attending funerals of doctors who gave her six months to live; the two old sisters who pleaded with the doctor not to tell their third sister that she had extreme cancer, and was going to die because they said she would not be able to stand it. Likewise the third sister, who came to know it was cancer by intuition, begged the doctor not to tell her sisters, whom she was convinced would fall to bits if they knew.

The teen-aged boy in hospital, who knew he had a fatal form of cancer, and faced it with supreme courage, and did everything in his power to keep it from his parents. But the parents had been told, and were keeping it from him! Blindman's buff to the very end, which wasted their chance to share and help the young man's plight. Those last months were made more hollow and empty for both.

It is a matter of whether we care, and understand people. By and large, people are bigger than we give them credit for being. The great majority, even those with no religious faith, are braver than we ever expect, and often resent being kept in ignorance and being nannied along by a doctor. It is not fair to fill patients up with a pack of lies, and fail to give them a chance to show the stuff they have in them. If doctors baby them along all the time, they will not get co-operation out of them. This is terribly important in the postoperative period in a cancer case. Once the patient finds out a doctor has been lying in response to direct questions, in order to pussyfoot him along, a ghastly harvest of unnecessary fears may result. He will, in the turmoil of his mind, cease to believe even the truthful optimistic hopes of his prognosis. Mutual trust and credulity has been destroyed to a point where he can no longer believe anything or anybody. In his well of loneliness, the doctor has made it impossible for anyone to reach him. Fear of the unknown is very much greater than the fear of the known. So-called "justifiable distortion of the medical truth" may lead to complete loss of confidence, and even to contempt.

This is of course so elementary that it might not be thought worth mentioning, but there are some very elementary people about. The technician in the operating theatre sees so little of the patient, except for when he is unconscious, that he is sometimes the worst judge of the psychology of the patient. Besides, we never present the same self twice when we go for an interview with a doctor, a parson, or a prospective employer. Time and again it is the radiotherapist who understands far more of the mentality of cancer patients than anyone else, and this is, no doubt, because he has to see so much more of the patient, and needs the patient's co-operation. Many radiotherapists have told me that, given two patients with roughly the same condition and prognosis, and give them the same treatment, so often the one with faith, or even a crude desire to get well, survives, and the pessimist and faithless, who may have started off with a better prognosis, does not respond so well, and often mysteriously dies. One world famous radiotherapist remarked to me that for all he knew, the recovery of the one may not have had anything much to do with his treatment, but may have been the mystery of spontaneous regression. As Pyrrho has said, "We cannot even be sure that we are not sure."

May I repeat then that whilst England, or any other country, is kept in dreadful ignorance of the progress of research, and the success of modern treatments, we must continue to perpetrate a cascade of lies and complete ignorance on the subject of cancer. Give the nation a healthy understanding of the successful cases, a healthy appreciation that long-term success depends on patient-to-doctor co-operation, and individual faith, and we shall then be able to tell the patient what is wrong with him. This will establish a far more healthy confidence in the medical profession, which is a very great profession.

I hope to show you that Cancer Anonymous is a new way

of thinking, acting, and feeling about the whole problem of cancer. It is a new concept which involves more responsibilities, going deep into the heart of human suffering. Responsibilities far beyond fund raising, public education, research and hospitalisation—namely, the spiritual faith and battling courage of the poor suffering individual and his welfare in terms of human kindness, especially in the hopeless cases.

If the mind, subject to great stress and worry, can upset the pituitary, and if in turn this can create an imbalance of the intercellular fluids, surely it is important that the patient should be encouraged to set his mind at unity, and at equilibrium with God, so that the divine healing processes can be brought to bear upon the pituitary, and thence to the rest of the body. To get this kind of co-operation from the patient, he needs to be brought into the confidence of the doctor.

If this new Christ-centred concept of the cancer problem can be spread wide enough to raise the confident hope and fighting courage of a potential patient, it will mean that when he is ill he can be told frankly what his trouble is if it happens to be cancer, without fear that he will wish to curl up and die. It will enable him to summon up every antibody within him—spiritual and material—to help the surgeon to win the battle in the operating theatre, to say nothing of the radiotherapy clinic. *No one ought to underestimate the power of the will to live.* No one ought to predict the actual death of a desperately ill patient, for who can tell what might happen . . . spontaneous regression, or some new "cure" may be discovered, or the miracle of divine healing may take place . . . who really knows?

There is every possible reason for breaking through the barrier of silence about cancer and raising the flag and letting the world know about the cures and the courage to endure. Make no mistake about it, many forms of cancer can be cured. One of the keys to success is to report the symptoms at an early stage, and for the local doctor to recognise it and take it seriously, applying all the tests. People will not report early if they do not know the symptoms and while the iron curtain of silence about cures is maintained. The second key is to be determined that with God's help and with a qualified doctor you will never give in.

I hope that Cancer Anonymous will be able to inspire a series of cancer-detection clinics up and down the country, where people can go for an annual checkup, receiving all the tests that are available today; namely a total physical examination, with minute care, from top to bottom, chest X ray, blood test, urine test, biopsy of any surface growth, rectal and vaginal examination with a proctoscope and sigmoidscope, and the smear test.

The seven warning signals are:

(1) Discharge or unusual bleeding from any body opening.

(2) Any sore that does not heal.

(3) Nagging hoarseness or cough.

(4) Growth or thickening in the breast or elsewhere.

(5) Extreme changes in warts or moles.

(6) Radical changes in normal bowel habits.

(7) Swallowing difficulty or persistent indigestion.

The best of local doctors are always on the lookout for cancer, and some say 40 per cent of their training in hospitals is to teach them to "spot" cancer. This is a very significant fact. Thus the doctors are the outriders of the hospitals, surgeons, and radiotherapy departments. If the patient will steer clear of quacks and will only see his doctor regularly and be quite frank with him, many, many more cases will be cured. It really should not be necessary for the public to know too much about the symptoms, but, on the other hand, posters tell the world the symptoms of venereal disease, and books tell the ordinary mother the symptoms of her children's possible complaints.

There has been such a taboo about cancer that it has created a vicious circle of defeat that has killed all hope, even in the face of a doctor's reassurances at the bedside.

Of course, there are some people who like to believe the worst and have no intention from the start of believing the doctor's reassurances, and no matter what he says, they "know it is fatal." With most patients, that cynical disbelieving voice rises up within them to discredit what the doctor says. This happens at the time of the interview or during that agonising period of depression before or after the operation.

The voice inside says: "He thinks I am a fool or a 'Worry guts' or can't take it, so he soft-soaps me." "He is just being kind and breaking it to me gently." "He thinks that I don't know that a friend of mine died of this." "I know perfectly well that for his own pride's sake he would never admit that all his patients were failures. Oh, if only he could give me the name of one single person who has been cured, I would take courage and believe his reassurances. It is all so vague when he tells me that large numbers of patients do recover and that I would be surprised if I knew the names of certain well-known people alive today who are cured cancer patients."

The tragedy, of course, is that medical etiquette prevents him and the hospital from giving any names. Here Cancer Anonymous can come to the rescue of hospitals and doctors.

So the argument goes on in the mind of the patient and the relatives and the public. Often we think the patient is in blissful ignorance of the fact that he has cancer, but when you lie in bed you have ears at the back of your head and develop a sixth sense for putting two and two together. Besides, most people crawl to the end of their bed to read the notes, or they ask a visitor to do so for them. Relatives are usually told, and they are the worst people at lying to those who know them so well.

Thus by devious routes the truth of what is feared is learned and yet the other side of the picture is not known— namely, that cancer can be cured or endured and that this can happen in many different ways.

It is vital, not merely for the peace of mind of the patient but for the success of the treatment, that the patient should know of and believe in those cures. It is vital that the patient should have found Christian courage. The fighting spirit can release new life-giving energies which will assist the surgeon and radiologist.

Who knows if man cannot, by his own effort with God's help, release a fresh supply of hormones, antibodies, or a new chemical balance which will attack that growth bump on the chromosome within the cancer cell. Who knows if man cannot release a chemical balance so that the nucleo-proteins, which control cell characteristics, become resistant to some carcinogenic virus? Is this the secret of spontaneous regression or faith healing? Is this how God answers prayer? Many apparently hopeless cases do live on.

Even in the face of the most dire suffering or bitter oppression experienced in our world, mankind must never lose hope. *Hope is the most precious possession any of us can have. Coupled with courage it can work wonders.* The embittered cynic says we must not raise false hopes and ends by killing all hopes.

Yes, hope and courage are very vital in the situation, for while there is hope, there is life enough for the next day and that day may be the turning point. Sheer determination can "help" to beat this crab which seeks to destroy the body. May I repeat—courage is something you sweat out daily with God and is inspired by Christ.

Now the infant prodigy of my own mind is to germinate

the idea of Cancer Anonymous as a means of running up the flag of victory for all to see, and to bring renewed physical help, renewed hope, and Christian encouragement to the sufferer and the fearful. Cancer Anonymous teaches the will to live and overcome, or in the last resort to die bravely and gracefully because there is another world.

Will I succeed in lighting this flame and setting victorious cancer patients to work for one another . . . in setting the healthy to give of their money, time, brains, talents, and influence to improve welfare, religious, and medical facilities?

Will I be defeated by the iron curtain of secrecy or by overcautious sections of the medical profession?

Will people or societies misunderstand what I am driving at and distort what could be of immense help to humanity because they are jealous or hard-boiled?

The Cancer Anonymous concept is no mechanical organisation. Cancer Anonymous, as I see it, could be grafted on to any relief society in any country or to any hospital, or church. Its philosophy is the handmaid of the doctor, the hospital, and all who seek to help in this field.

You can guess that I stole the title from "Alcoholics Anonymous" which has done such wonderful work for those afflicted with drink. In essence, Alcoholics Anonymous is not a set of well-meaning people helping the drinkers, but alcoholics helping fellow alcoholics. They are anonymous for various reasons, chiefly because drunkenness is something to be ashamed of.

Cancer Anonymous is a way of thinking about cancer with a positive spiritual foundation. It says, in effect, that the only hope for man's spirit and courage in the face of cancer is to find strength in God. Peace of soul drawn from Christ gives the power to fight and endure, and takes the sting out of death. It seeks to build the courage of the individual by extending to him a proper balanced knowledge about cancer and the many witnesses of living, happy, grateful, cured ex-patients. It waves the banner of victory for him to follow. It injects into all work for cancer the all-important thought that the man's own personal struggle is as vital to the surgeon and radiotherapist as any amount of scientific skill. To gain this determination Cancer Anonymous witnesses must bring to him, as part of his everyday thinking, the sure knowledge that there are cured cancer patients, that there are others who are enduring it, that there are others who have fought a good fight, but because of our limited medical knowledge have passed on to that other world. This passing into another world is not to be feared but accepted with grace and peace. Death is but a gentle step from darkness to light.

In essence Cancer Anonymous becomes the very opposite of anonymous and is the vehicle by which patients, especially cured patients, show their gratitude by publicly making known their cancer victory and by pledging themselves to the many ideals of Cancer Anonymous in order that they may do what they can for others in terms of spiritual things and the milk of human kindness. This is no mechanical organisation, but, like Christianity, it is a way of living and acting and believing. It commands your loyalty, loyalty based on gratitude and a desire to help others. It starts by being anonymous and ends by being publicly known. It has to be anonymous to start. You go to your doctor, or your parson, or to one of our information offices, and you do not expect others to learn personal details about you. You are assured that if you do get well you are not going to be bathed in a bath of publicity. You can serve Cancer Anonymous, if you are so inclined, as a humble, unknown person, but you are encouraged, if you are strong enough, to come out in the open. Some ludicrous people, who believe in making known victory, are not mentally adult enough to understand the necessity for the anonymous element in Cancer Anonymous, but, of course, the world is full of people who are so blind that they will not see truth, even when it is sticking out a mile. I am concerned for the protection of patients and relatives.

With gentleness they are approached under the banner of secret confidence anonymously and drawn into an unseen fellowship of determined people anxious to live out the Christian faith even in the face of suffering. As they are able, they are inspired to pass through the barrier and protection of "Anonymous" to become witnesses and visitors to those in like distress, if they are strong enough.

I want the message or germ behind Cancer Anonymous to say to a patient: "Look, you are cured or you have learned to endure it. Can you not do something to help others locally or through some central organisation? First, let's run up the flag of victory to help kill the idea that cancer means death. Your witness breaking through the silence of anonymity will be of great value to others. They need proof—attested proof—before they will allow themselves to hope. Give them that gleam of hope even before they fall ill.

"Tell your doctor he can use your name—tear up the idea of anonymity if you feel strong enough. If you feel able, offer yourself at a hospital as a visitor, pledging your word that you will never broadcast what will downcast. Seek out the worried relatives of some newly afflicted person and inspire them to surround their patient with prayer, courage, and optimism. See to it that your cancer society in whatever country you live has the heart to help in spiritual as well as practical ways, with money and facilities for the many tragic cases. Help those organisations to raise money and make sure that it is spent in the right way. Hospitals are crying out for patients who will return alive and well in order to share their victory with the forlorn and dejected. There is a need for those who have mastered their disabilities to become Cancer Anonymous witnesses to someone else who, having just gone through an operation, is worried about the conquest and training of his disabled body.

"Work to educate and raise the morale of the public. Win your own battle back to the stream of life by looking forward to the day when you can be of some little service to another or to relatives. Nothing like looking ahead and outside of yourself! Be wholeheartedly determined to live and it may give you the courage to count yourself yet one more Cancer Anonymous witness, and pray for this band of workers, although we may never meet."

I want the message or germ behind Cancer Anonymous to say to relatives all that this book has been trying to say. Never, never give up hope. Never be afraid of taking a second opinion. Talk the matter over openly with your doctor, and even if, medically, the case is pronounced hopeless, there may yet be that unknown regression which baffles all of us. Maybe your private doctor gives the impression that he can do no more, possibly he may not wish to take any more money. It is then that people pass into the hands of quacks who will bleed their patients of money in a last frantic endeavour to stem the tide. It is here that Cancer Anonymous could possibly help to adjust that patient for the day when we step into "another room." Be sure to be on your guard against quacks, especially at the beginning when you first learn of the disease, lest you waste valuable days before proper treatment is begun.

I would ask you to find some clergyman or priest who understands this problem, who can lead you and your loved one to a spiritual faith in quietness and confidence, which knows deep down that the sufferings of this present time are not worthy to be compared with the glories which shall be revealed hereafter. In the face of death, we need a faith so living that death loses its sting and we know we are merely passing into another room. There your loved one, at last, will be free of all pain, and in that heavenly state he would not have you spoil the rest of your journey in this world by being overcome with grief. Death, to a Christian, has not the sting it has to the pagan.

I want the message and ideal of Cancer Anonymous to be learned by all Christian leaders so that they learn to understand this cancer problem and are inspired to become Cancer Anonymous counsellors. Cancer Anonymous could be the umbrella to secure reforms where they are needed in various countries. It could be a whip to the conscience of nations to secure money for existing societies, and a means of keeping always before those societies and the medical profession the spiritual needs of the individual patient. Thus the relatives and the healthy have their part to play in Cancer Anonymous, and many such people without a membership will help with this book. I hope that cancer societies, like societies for the blind and limbless, will draw their enthusiasm and life blood not solely from a set of healthy organisers but from the enthusiastic ranks of the many Cancer Anonymous ex-patient witnesses. Do not imagine that Cancer Anonymous proposes get-togethers of ex-cancer patients who might compare notes on so complex a disease! I do hope to hold united services of thanksgiving in churches for ex-cancer patients, and such services, well advertised, should serve as an inspiration to others.

I am interested in:

(a) Christian faith, hope and courage.

(b) Welfare for the afflicted.

(c) Reforms and new facilities where they are needed in whatever country.

As a result of one article in *Church Illustrated* in December 1955, which was also reproduced in various American magazines, I get a steady flow of letters, and in time we shall build up an increasing army of victorious witnesses for Cancer Anonymous, who will be praying and working for our concept, and many will find the courage to break through the anonymous screen to serve their fellow men in person or in print. I have issued a booklet of victorious case histories and I hope to produce a convincing colour film to bring hope and courage entitled *Cancer Can Be Cured or Endured*, but this will need a sponsor and co-operation of cancer societies and doctors.

I launched the idea of Cancer Anonymous for the first time in November 1955 when preaching at the American Episcopal cathedral in Avenue George-V in Paris. Later, in January 1956, after consulting Dr. Cuthbert Bardsley, then Bishop of Croydon, I called a meeting at the English-Speaking Union of matrons and almoners (social-service officers) from the London hospitals, and Canon Bryan Green took the chair to enable me to explain the many ramifications and to invite ideas. I was greatly encouraged by the warm reception given by all—especially by the bishop, the National Society for Cancer Relief, and the Marie Curie Foundation.

The first public meeting I addressed in England on the subject of Cancer Anonymous was the Bournemouth Rotary luncheon on March 5, 1956, and *Life* magazine of America sent reporters and photographers. It is obvious on all sides that there is a tremendous interest in and need for such a concept or ideal and it will undoubtedly snowball into activity in many countries.

The churches, Rotary, and Lions International with their emphasis on social service could play a great part, with results beneficial not merely to their members when in need but to the whole community. Here are groups of sane, levelheaded men who could face squarely the menace of cancer and see to it that at least one member in their fellowship is appointed as the C. A. counsellor. He would then be the one in their midst who kept himself well informed on the subject and thus be in a position to help patients and relatives in time of need. I would stress that although a man or woman struck down by this wretched disease is usually in need of money and material help, the most important help which Cancer Anonymous can bring is in terms of spiritual strength and courage.

Cancer brings a depression all its own. Bereft of health, home, office, and the good things of life, and lying in a hospital bed, there is little else to lay hands on but God Himself and the knowledge that one has a few friends in this world who are loyal and are praying that courage will not fail. It is comforting to know that friends will look after our worrying dependents.

What a relief it would be to know that friends like a local Cancer Anonymous group were watching over you with the relatives to see that the best treatment was being obtained. If the word "terminal" was pronounced and the hospital bed was needed, it would be grand to know that Cancer Anonymous followed you home with the provision of special bandages and a little financial subsidy and advice to others in the household. What a wonderful job the Women's Voluntary Service did in war time for air raid casualties and evacuees! Thank God for the throat-cancer clubs of ex-patients who teach one another how to speak again. In America the American Cancer Society is increasingly looking after the needs of the individual patient . . . there is a needed swing to welfare.

I have been asked to write a series of small booklets for use on different occasions, in the hospital or the home, giving encouragement to different types of patients with practical hints on how to live with the particular disability.

The idea behind this is the Cancer Anonymous witness in print, for not every cured patient can face frequent visits to a hospital ward to give personal advice and help. When I come home from a hospital visit I sometimes have to pray my sadness away.

The titles suggested for these booklets are: *So Now They Have Told You, The Surgeon Needs Your Help, Adjusted to Our Restrictions, Cancer Anonymous Victories Case Histories, Cancer Can Be Cured or Endured, Courage and God, A Cancer Anonymous Counsellor.*

The fellowship of Cancer Anonymous has grown and we have many helpful case histories to draw upon in order to run up the flag of victory, so that a new hope will arise in the hearts of men. The motto is, "Cancer can be cured or endured."

Who will pay for the printing, distribution, and postage I do not know, since I have enough financial burdens in connection with the Dawn Trust and Greystoke to weigh me down for at least ten years, and I have no desire to handle an appeal or be stifled with mountains of office work.

But the way is already opening up and there are forth-coming, ex-cancer patients and sympathisers, with busi-ness and organising experience, or with money or talents, whom I can inspire to put the many aspects of Cancer Anonymous into world-wide operation. I only need a few men of wealth, influence, organising ability, and positive faith, to catch my vision of what the Cancer Anonymous concepts could do for the world, and a flood tide of good would arise.

At present I am content to have a small bank account in England and Los Angeles, and hope that one day it will grow large enough to cover the printing of leaflets and the giving of this book to the sick and poor. Large enough to maintain an advice bureau and inspire, in England, a British Cancer Society.

Meanwhile the idea is gaining momentum and I have

more letters than I can effectively deal with. More and more ex-cancer patients have been offering themselves to their local hospitals as Cancer Anonymous witnesses. In fact, I am finding increasingly that cancer patients are only too anxious to help spread the news of victory and courage in their own circle, once they realise the good it will do for others.

So often, when a patient has a successful operation, he is told that of course it was not really "malignant." This is probably done lest he should worry, whereas it gives rise to the fallacy that those who die had cancer and that those who live did not really have it. From this they imagine the worst possible picture, whereas many ex-cancer patients are living happy useful lives.

In America it is possible to obtain regular check-ups against cancer if anyone desires to have them, but in England such an idea would be greeted with derision by many in the medical profession. There is only one check clinic in the whole of England, and this is at a leading London hospital, where on Tuesday afternoons at 2:30 P.M. anyone may turn up without an introduction card. One afternoon a week, in only one hospital! In my opinion an efficient easy system will have to come into operation in every country. The usual excuse against cancer-check clinics and educating the public as to the symptoms is that it might create alarm and despondency, but that is just begging the question. As yet there is no real check till the outward and visible signs appear of an inward and cellular disorder, but there are known indications.

In the fight against T.B., the mass X-ray clinics, where people can go free of charge and have a picture taken, have done a superb job. It was, at first, a revolutionary step which was bitterly opposed by some. I would like to see in every city a confidential cancer office set up so that the fearful, the ill, and the ex-patient could drop in without

formality or publicity and be advised by a trained nurse
about the latest tests and what to do. It would have a little
"Red" door and a listed telephone number under Cancer
Anonymous. From this local rally point would stem the
team of volunteers making and distributing comforts,
flowers, and bandages, etc., to the sick in hospital and
home. *Total cancer care* is what I am driving at, including
the spiritual healing of the mind. Mere factual education
would be replaced by the thought that people do care
about you when you are ill with cancer. A revolutionary
idea, but it would help many people and help track down
the disease in the early stages. One day I hope that a grateful Cancer Anonymous enthusiast will pay for a series of
these care offices, as well as other reforms, and thus set a
new fashion in many a country.

In many cities, particularly in America, you can dial AA
on the phone and quickly receive help. I would like to see
a Cancer Anonymous call number in big cities, paid for by
the city council or someone and controlled by the medical
officer of health. Only in one city in Britain—Hull—has this
been tried out. There you could dial the cancer number
and listen to a three-minute recorded talk on the subject,
which was varied every week under doctors' supervision.
In the first few months' trial ten thousand phone calls were
received. The service was paid for and provided by the
Marie Curie Foundation, which is doing such excellent
work and has homes for terminal cancer patients. These
telephone talks, written by a panel of doctors, are now
available in booklet form. This idea could be extended to a
twenty-four-hour personal service based on confidential
cancer offices in big cities. In some countries they already
have a great deal of wonderful work going on which could
be shared internationally. I visualise the day when some
influential Cancer Anonymous enthusiast in Britain or
elsewhere will finance the deployment of these basic con-

CANCER ANONYMOUS 217

ceptions even from a humanitarian point of view, and promote a counsellor-training plan for Christian leaders who would assist each local confidential cancer office and build teams of cancer-cured witnesses who would help. The volume of letters which I receive from suffering patients and worried relatives in Britain and America make it clear to me that a chain of information offices will meet a great need but that it all costs money, time, and thought, to say nothing of medical backing and a spirit of co-operation between cancer societies.

It does not need much imagination on the part of the British to look out on the field of cancer and what is being done about it, to realise that all is not well. Did you know that we have no national policy towards cancer in the clinical and welfare fields, no detection clinics, no modern hospitals, no specialised-treatment clinics, no advice bureaux, and no united society? Pick up a magazine, and we find four competing advertisements appealing for funds, and at the same time we are conscious that the National Health spends a great deal of money in the field of cancer. Those four societies are as follows:

Two Research: Imperial Cancer Research Fund, which believes in and operates fundamental research in its own buildings, and these buildings need drastic rebuilding in the centre of London.

British Empire Cancer Campaign: Originally a rival, with a very similar name. It spends money on research anywhere in the old Empire.

British brains are exported all over the world, and are found in charge of research and clinical institutions, because we lack the facilities to keep them in Britain. We have practically no clinical research, and are in danger of allowing basic fundamental research to build walls around itself. We have no central cancer hospital to attract the kind of brains that are needed in total cancer care. In fact there is a danger that radiotherapy may be separated from even the Royal Marsden Hospital.

Two societies working in the field of welfare: The National Society for Cancer Relief, which gives the money it collects from advertisement appeals, to almoners of hospitals, in grants, who in turn dispense it to the needy. They do a wonderful work in a limited field, with limited resources. Last year they gave away sixty thousand pounds.

The Marie Curie Foundation, which spreads the money it collects, so far, on three homes for the incurables. Therefore it does a wonderful work in a limited field, with limited resources.

Compare all this for one moment with the vast crescendo of suffering in our land, and then look at Canada or America, and you will work as I do, that one day there will dawn a new era in Britain, a willingness on the part of all these different societies, peoples, and persons, to weld themselves together, without losing their precious individuality. My dream is to inspire the creation of a united BRITISH CANCER SOCIETY, worthy of a nation of administrators. It would take many pages for me to explain what such a society could do for Britain, to put this country on a war footing, so that we were organised at least as well as the Canadian Cancer Society and the American Cancer Society.

Some of us in Cancer Anonymous, with our many friends in high places, in Parliament and in the medical profession, are doing the donkeywork towards bringing societies and personalities together.

Meanwhile our nation is sick and tired of competing public appeals for cancer, not merely because it is thoroughly muddled by the situation, but because it is never told of any stage of progress. It is left to newspaper reporters to pick up bits to throw to the public. It is left to M.P.s to ask a few questions in the House, and hear the

hasty assurances of a Minister of Health. The public is tired
of these appeals because it sees no evidence of improvement of clinical facilities, no policy of detection clinics,
or checkup centres. It sees no improvement in the welfare conditions for suffering humanity. The average man
feels that if he has paid his National Health and contrib-
uted towards cancer appeals, he has a right to expect to
hear a little bit about the progress of research, to see
better detection and treatment conditions, and better
facilities of welfare for the sufferers of today. The general
public is beginning to realise that one in every four persons
is attacked by this disease, in one form or another, and
that an ever widening circle of relations suffer as a result.
The public is beginning to realise, through the activity of
Cancer Anonymous, that thousands suffer and die without
knowing it was cancer, without being given a chance to
fight back, or with just a haunting suspicion which is
cradled in secret and in misery. Cancer, like fear, is best
fought out in the daylight, with patient co-operation.
Many suffer unnecessarily, many are cured, and many
more could be cured, or have their burdens lightened. The
public is beginning to hear whispers of how dissatisfied the
medical profession is with every aspect of cancer care.

Cancer Anonymous works on a cell system of a gradual
increase of the number of men and women in high and
lowly positions, in Parliament, hospitals, churches, busi-
nesses and clubs, who spontaneously use their influence
as self-appointed workers to bring about a change in attitude and in conditions till we all become conscious of the
vital necessity and priority of total cancer care and the
milk of human kindness.

Let us have a "divine discontent," with conditions as
they are, lest complacency within the medical field becomes the counterpart to apathy in the general public.
When we have done all that we can do, it still is not

enough. Even if we improve the treatment conditions, and develop clinical research, we should still be faced with the heart of the trouble, namely the domestic chaos that is caused when cancer knocks at the door.

Is it surprising therefore that Cancer Anonymous has so many "friends at court" in high and low places, who will now stir themselves to mould public opinion and help forward our concepts? They are to be found in every walk of life, and the people shall be heard in the seats of the mighty for the sake of the present generation.

Will you be a "friend at court" in one way or another, and think up some way of helping Cancer Anonymous and of stimulating public opinion in the nation or in some hospital, as a self-appointed good cell?

Meanwhile the work of the Cancer Anonymous Advice Service must go on, for the suffering, the lonely, the panic-stricken relatives, the tired and the fearful who line the hospital benches as broken cogs in a vast machine. This bureau is the spearhead of publicity for reforms. It is in close touch with doctors, almoners, hospitals, and welfare societies, and has a team of ex-patients. It has already been instrumental in saving lives.

Cancer Anonymous has a story of victory and endurance to tell through its members, which could bring new heart into the nation, and it has the warm friendly backing of many of the top cancer specialists.

Up till now Dawn Trust has carried the work of Cancer Anonymous, in addition to its religious and educational film work. This is an extra burden, but the future may alter the position. With the help of my medical conspirators, who are among the most enlightened in the medical profession, I am not only working and pulling strings to weld together a federated BRITISH CANCER SOCIETY, but trying to inspire the building of a headquarters for the same, which would be the finest cancer centre and cancer hospital, right in the centre of London. There is a site available. It would need eight million pounds to create it, but at least the British public would at long last see something for their money, in the face of the giant disease of our day and generation. The public likes to see tangible results, and not academic talk and political fob-off. We can devote millions for defence against war, and we can even be up to date enough to adjust ourselves to atomic war. It takes a bit of doing for the Old School Tie, who still wish wars were fought on horseback. It will take a bit of doing to adjust the Old School Tie to fight cancer, with total cancer care, using all that atomic energy and chemotherapy can afford.

Let me dream a while with you. . . . I see on this site a standing memorial to all who have died or suffered from cancer during this present twentieth century. I see not a Florence Nightingale hospital, but an ultramodern building, which will become the pulsating brain of Britain in the field of cancer. Let us call it the BRITISH CANCER HOSPITAL, with a teaching staff drawn from the present Co-operating Hospitals scheme. Famous surgeons and doctors will be attracted to it, because of its fabulous facilities, which will be second to none. Total cancer care will be a foregone conclusion; surgery, radiotherapy, chemotherapy, and all the new treatments. There will be no trouble about nurses and voluntary staff. Indeed they will all be forthcoming, because it will be a twentieth-century hospital, with an eager Elizabethan spirit. In the very heart of it there will be a truly inspirational chapel, and the healing services of the churches will be very much in evidence. The whole *décor* will strike a new line for hospitals. We would invent a new word for the Outpatients' Department, which would not resemble a European third-class railway carriage, with gruff officials. Into these consulting rooms ill patients could come, with or without a letter of introduction, any day of the week. The treatment facilities would actually work at weekends; a staggering innovation.

It goes without saying that the operating theatres, electrical departments, wards, and private rooms would have the finest equipment. Talking of wards, there would be experimental wards for voluntary desperately ill patients, for chemotherapy and metabolic treatments. These wards would be closely linked with the Research Wing, and thus clinical research would blossom as a rose. The whole hospital would have a two-way traffic, at close quarters with the Imperial Cancer Laboratory in Lincoln's Inn. Even the B.E.C.C. would soon be sponsoring much of the research work.

The second most important wing would be the DETECTION CLINIC, where the apparently well could come for their annual checkups, and be studied scientifically. Here also anyone could come without formality, for an emergency checkup, or a double checkup. This would be closely linked with the Advice Bureau and Welfare Wing. Here would be found the offices of the main societies interested in this work. They would build and train a national volunteer force, who would be involved in public education, professional education, and the needs of the patient and community. They would make the special dressings, and other comforts in hospital and home. Their voluntary workers, dressed in yellow, would be seen around the wards, bringing hope to individuals, solving their domestic problems, and arranging flowers from the BRITISH CANCER SOCIETY at the bedside of every new patient. They would assist the almoners and home-help organisations on a voluntary basis or part time.

The august names in the medical profession would be seen on the Board, doing their job to co-ordinate research, treatment, teaching, education and welfare. There would be no divorce between doctors and clergy, no divorce be-

tween doctors and lay people, either in the hospital or in
the BRITISH CANCER SOCIETY. There would be one
month—April—when a united effort for funds would be
made, and there would be an agreed scale of distribution
to the four or five objectives, both regionally and nation-
ally.

Shall we call this "The main dream," and it is not so far,
because there are many signs that the tide is beginning to
turn, even in dear old Britain. We may have to start with
merely a detection clinic on this side, to be followed by a
radiotherapy unit, rather than see this far out in the sub-
urbs of London.

All of this is vital to Britain, but if any should chance to
read this from other countries, there are many general reforms that we should be interested in, for we cannot be
concerned, in Cancer Anonymous, with the needs of the
individual, without examining what is medically available
to him.

I sincerely look forward to the day, through pressure of
public opinion as a result of this book when some much
needed reforms come into operation. Reforms which
might otherwise take years of political lobbying. There are
many important reforms or trends which I consider to be
vital for any country. 1) An accurate CANCER REGIS-
TRY in every hospital, in order to keep track of patients
and observe the success or otherwise of various forms of
treatments with different types of patients. The register
would have a welfare slant. 2) A CANCER PANEL or
FORUM of specialists in the main hospitals where experience and knowledge is pooled. Here the disease is treated
as a whole instead of just being treated in one department
without the pooled examination of the case in the light of
the CANCER REGISTRY. In teaching hospitals this is
sometimes known as the TUMOR CONFERENCE which
examines and discusses cases and the next treatment. This

is sometimes devastating for the doctors and surgeons in the presence of students, but it is stimulating! 3) A TISSUE COMMITTEE in every hospital which checks back on everything which comes out of the operating room. It is a guide for and check on a surgeon for the hospital committee. 4) A series of CANCER HOSPITALS up and down every country, and the bigger ones would have two extra wings—one for predetection where well people are studied for their own benefit and for science—one for fundamental research. The hospital should have metabolic experimental research wards of volunteer desperate cases. The close proximity of research and clinical treatment will produce the much needed CLINICAL RESEARCH WORKERS. 6) A series of smaller local CANCER OFFICES with a threefold constitution—medical, secular, and spiritual. The medical side would be the local outrider of the proper cancer hospital and the link with the busy general doctor. This could be the cancer-detection clinic for annual and urgent checkups. The secular side would be the local information, fund raising, relief and comfort dispensing of the combined national cancer societies, who ought to work in harmony. The spiritual side would be where Cancer Anonymous counsellors, with a firmly based personal faith, run a service to individuals and have on call a host of victorious brave Cancer Anonymous witnesses, i.e., cured patients. 7) An urgent PRIORITY for CANCER cases for beds, treatments, operations, and radio- or chemotherapy. 8) Adequate PROVISION for the TERMINAL CASES, in the way of institutions and a home service with a follow through welfare.

It is right that we should give heartily to cancer research for the benefit of the patient of tomorrow, but it is also right that we should give tremendously for the treatment, relief, welfare services, and spiritual care of the patients of today, especially the slow terminal cases. The concept, which, for want of any other omnibus name, I call Cancer Anonymous, pleads that you should give your money in the big cancer fund-raising drives and at some time see that it is spent right. As a Christian philosophy it pleads that in addition to money giving you should give your time as a volunteer for your local cancer group or society.

Young men dream dreams and old men see visions, but I long for the day when "Total Cancer Care" outside and inside hospitals is the order of the day. So long as the spirit of my concept is even partially absorbed by some group, I am happy.

In the early days of T.B. mass-X ray free clinics, a certain person donated one and he was asked if he would come and declare it open and be the first to have his "picture" taken. He duly arrived, and when the picture was developed they found he had cancer of the lung in the early stages, and his life was saved. Those who opposed mass T.B. X rays were put to silence! This is only one case out of many, and the mass X rays for tuberculosis are helping us to track down cancer of the lung. A blood donor turned up at a hospital to give his blood, and the doctor happened to take the ESR test from a sample of the man's blood. The sedimentation rate was running at a colossal rate, so the fellow was examined and cancer piles were discovered. It took foresight and energy to put over the idea of mass-X ray free clinics and a few swift gifts cut down years of red tape. Could we not do as much against the great killer —cancer?

By all means let us build up vast sums for cancer-research projects in the hope of a cure, never losing sight of the fact that it may evolve from the work of some "hospital doctor" who is in touch with life as it is lived by humans. The common complaint by the man in the street is that, despite the millions spent on research and training, scientists have not come up with a cure. Will someone be brave enough to set up a Christian Cancer Research Fund to train and maintain chaplains in this field of human agony?

Cancer can be cured by the combination of medical science, positive faith, and human energy.

Cancer is not just a physical affliction in one corner of the body. It becomes a state of soul and mind just as much as of body.

In addition to curing its bodily roots, we must also eradicate its roots in the mind, otherwise cures or arrested cases will have warped minds. Cured patients will still weep in the darkness of their lives, instead of climbing on to the band wagon of life and making the most of every minute and returning to earn a living once again.

The surgeon succeeds in the operating theatre, but without the determined effort and faith of the patient all can be lost again, at least in the mind. If only Christian leaders and priests understood more of the cancer problem and the Cancer Anonymous concept, they could be of tremendous help. The afflicted are hungry for bread and we must take care lest we give them a stonelike cancer programme devoid of God.

Beneath the surface of millions of lives throughout the world, there is an ever-present pulsating fear of cancer which is destroying man's potential, robbing him of that happy lightness to his step and keeping him back from enjoying the full measure of the powers of attainment which are latent with him.

The toll of human worry which goes whistling down the wind is indeed one of the great problems of our day. We know that cancer is the major scourge of our generation . . . indeed, the more we know from science, the more we realise the extent of this disease and value man's puny efforts to battle with it.

But remember, a great deal of the suffering from cancer

is in the mind. It is all too easy for people to develop cancer of the mind . . . a sort of phobia . . . which can rot their whole perspective if they let their dark imaginings go unchecked beneath the surface.

Cancer Anonymous pledges itself, by every breath of the lives of those who believe in it, to beat the cancer mental phobia so that healthy, soundly based courage is born again right in the midst of fear. It is not enough to say: "Don't worry, it may never happen to you," for when fear strikes the human breast it needs argument, facts, and reasonings based on solid foundations.

So Cancer Anonymous seeks to raise the knowledge of God and what is being done by doctors—to raise the knowledge of the many cases of victory or courageous endurance —and pleads that it is vital for those who have the slightest reason to doubt or fear to go at once to a doctor. That there are not adequate check clinics we know, but in time conditions will improve as the conscience of nations stirs and science finds a way.

We do not need a psychologist to tell us that people fear cancer and adopt the "roll-up-and-die" technique merely because of defeatist publicity or lack of "guts."

The empty pocketbook is in many cases the underlying factor. "How can I pay for expensive treatment?" "How can I afford to convalesce?" "How can I afford to be away from work as the breadwinner?" "If I recover, will I ever be well enough to earn my own living or to walk, swim, and enjoy life?" It is these questions which hold people back from reporting early and which cause people to weep in their beds in hospital.

I know, from my own experience, that I wanted to know of cures, and yet not just cures, but of those who were able to work and play games again. Four months after my operation I played squash with my wife and my son, and, after six months, skied in St. Moritz. This was more for the cure of my mind than anything else. If a man knew there was hope of a cure, it would take the sting out of the financial worry and the cancer depression. If he knew cures also depended on early reporting, he might take advice quickly.

A very great friend of mine who is a cancer doctor told me that he did not agree with Cancer Anonymous, and that I was all wrong to raise people's hopes. I smart under the lash of his cynical outlook when all of us know so little of the actual process of healing within the human body, and while the patient is prepared to fight there may yet dawn another day.

Man's destiny in his fight against the elements is his ability to hang on. No one knows for sure who will live or who will die of the various forms of cancer. Is there really such a thing as incurable cancer? Surely it is that some forms of cancer we do not yet know how to cure, and that we must not rule out the strange miracle of self-limiting cancer—or, to put it another way, the rise of antibodies from within, or a self-readjustment of the cellular balances.

The patient has his part to play, and it is well for him to promise the doctor that this will be done step by step.

Here are a number of victorious case histories from my Cancer Anonymous postbag which may serve to encourage you on one point or another:

Dear Mr. Hession,

Thank you for your letter. You may certainly have an account of my experience of cancer and use it in the course of your helpful ministrations.

In 1939, I consulted a doctor regarding a growth of the hardness of cement which covered my entire right chest. I had delayed seeing a doctor earlier because I was so terrified and because I was always hoping the growth would vanish! My doctor looked extremely serious and telephoned the London Hospital and made an appointment for me to see a specialist the same afternoon. The specialist also looked very serious and said I must have an operation next day. When I saw the word "Carcinoma" written on my case paper, I thought I should have broken down completely, as my mother had died in great suffering of this disease. The operation was considered very serious, as it necessitated stripping the wall of my chest and my armpit, but *I suffered practically nothing and was able to eat breakfast next morning and was playing tennis three months later*. The specialist saw me every three months for a time, then every six months, and for about the last eight years I have only been asked to attend the London Hospital once a year. On my last attendance in July 1955, the man who is in charge of cancer research called a few doctors, and these were his exact words: "I want you to see this patient—your nurses as well—because you are too fond of saying surgery is a waste of time in such cases as this. Miss Anderson had this operation in 1939 for carcinoma in an advanced stage and she has had no return." To me he said: "You are one of the lucky ones. I'll see you again in a year's time."

I was 41 when I had the operation. I am 58 now. Last year I retired from business but am active and well and look it. In fact, if you think my healthy appearance would give confidence to any terrified sufferer (as I was once) I shall be pleased to see them or to attend any of your meetings, but I am afraid I could never speak in public. Boredom is my greatest enemy now, as I miss a busy life.

If, at any time, I can help you, please let me know. I sold my portable typewriter a few months ago, so I cannot offer to type, but there may be other ways in which I can help you. I attend All Saints' Church, Blackheath, but the only activity there during the week is the Young Wives Fellowship and as I am not a wife, neither am I young, I am ineligible!

Frances E. Anderson

Dear Sir,

I can tell you of a "cured" cancer patient: my own mother. She is now seventy-three years of age, and had a very serious operation for the removal of a cancerous womb and ovaries over thirty years ago; she was so ill that the operation was not finished, and she had another about a year later to remove a small stump (so she was told then). Since then she has had no signs of cancer, and when she went into hospital a few years ago for some bladder trouble, we were told that they could find no traces at all of the old trouble: she is definitely cured. She had a fall last summer and does not go out now, but apart from some bronchitis she is quite well.

She says that she is quite willing to be used in any way to help sufferers, and would like to know how she can donate her body after death, for research purposes. She has always wished to do this, so perhaps you could let me know if such things are allowed, and how to go about it.

Violet E. Nelson

Dear Mr. Hession,

As one of your Cancer Anonymous workers at the office, my case may be of interest to others. I had cancer for four years before it was diagnosed. You know the ghastly details of those four black years, but it is now six years since I had my operations, and I am deeply grateful to the doctor and surgeons who eventually helped me. I can now appreciate so much more, life, my husband, and my child. It has all been well worth the effort to pull through. I attend the hospital every three months for a check-up.

Mrs. Kathleen Telfer

Dear Mr. Hession,

I was glad that you were able to use a picture of me on the front page of the Sunday *Graphic*, as part of the series of articles in which we Cancer Anonymous witnesses were able to give visual proof that after a drastic cancer operation we can enjoy life again.

You will remember that 6½ years ago, when I was three months' pregnant, they discovered I had cancer, and my breast was removed. My baby was born, and I was soon a busy housewife, bringing up my two children. I was pleased to see the happy picture in the paper of my six year old boy and my ten year old daughter, and I hope that the domestic scene was enough to bring courage and hope to those who fear the future, when faced with a like situation.

Mrs. Rosina Richardson

Here are five Cancer Witnesses:

Mr. Herbert Collins had a colostomy operation in 1951, and he is still a full-time entertainer and conjurer, and performs on television.

Mr. J. S. Marshall was operated on in 1949 for cancer of the throat, and is completely cured. Anyone, to meet him, would come to the conclusion that he was an attractive, handsome-looking man.

Mrs. P.B.A. had a cancer tumor removed from her stomach in 1952. She says she is now perfectly fit and well, and works hard. She was utterly without sympathy from her family, and says she kept going through faith in Christ, who suffered in Gethsemane alone.

Mrs. Elizabeth Corbett is a Superintendent at a Dr. Barnardo's Home, and she had a hysterectomy operation twelve years ago, and was given a maximum of two years to live. She works from 7 A.M. each day, until 9 or 10 P.M., and no one would know her secret disabilities since 1945.

Mrs. Florence Martin had a cancer operation twenty-five years ago at twenty-nine years of age, and has had a colostomy for that length of time. She has brought up a family of children, runs a guest home in the summer, and goes out to work in the winter. She swims, cycles, dances, and does everything a normal woman could do, and maybe more. She has had two or three other major operations since, but not for cancer, which she has taken in her stride. She still goes to the Royal Cancer Hospital for her annual checkup.

The following letters are typical of the sense of gratitude that so many people have even in the midst of illness:

Last August I was operated for a cancer, though at the time thought myself too young for such a disease to be in me. Anyway, I have found, through my illness, that there are many, many more who are far worse off, and I have so very much to be thankful for.

It brings me great joy to be able to write to you. I too am afflicted with this disease behind my left eye. I am married with two children and as you have experienced, Sir, it was a shock to my wife and myself to hear this news, but, by the grace of God, we have been strengthened and comforted to bear the burden.

During the last two years, I have had several operations and a concentrated course of X-ray on my face and through my left eye, and in the case of my last operation, on my neck and chest. I knew on that morning my whole future was held in the hand of God. I lay on a stretcher and just prayed with my whole being. I felt, too, that perfect calm and peace, never before experienced in my life, and by God's love and mercy, I was restored. I believe, Sir, that God can heal and that His mighty hand heals now as it did when the Master walked the earth, and although I have to go for a further operation on January 12th I believe God will strengthen and heal me.

My biggest problem is a constant one: I cannot at present do my normal work and I must admit for many years prior to my affliction, I was turning aside from God's laws. I feel now deep within me that for so great a blessing to be granted to one who has been so wayward, I should be doing some penitent work for God and for my fellow men, and although I pray for guidance the way does not seem too clear. I feel that in telling you in view of your experience and with the help of Cancer Anonymous, I may receive blessed guidance. I find to try and discuss it with anyone who has never been apparently saved by God's power is very difficult—that, Sir, is why the opportunity to write to you gives me such joy.

Please, Sir, would you send me details of Cancer Anonymous, and I do know, Sir, that I may ask you to remember me in your prayers when I have my next operation on January 12th.

Naturally, I wrote to him and when the day of his operation drew near I wrote again and scribbled a postscript telling him to hurry up and get well as we needed him, and that I would be praying for him.

This letter speaks for itself and shows how courageous people can be and how much they need true friends:

Dear Reverend Hession,

I thank you for your letter and for sending the *Church Illustrated* and found your article most interesting. As you say will-power and faith do a lot to help in cases such as ours. You ask if I would tell you of my own case, I will, but it must be understood that my name or address must not be published, the reason being I have been so hurt by people who I thought were my friends until they found out I had cancer, then they could not have been more afraid if one had the plague. Perhaps you in your calling have not met such people. I trust not. There is nothing to fear from us I am sure.

Well, here is my story. Many years ago, I went to my doctor and told him I was sure I had a growth in my stomach. He just laughed and said I was overworked and needed a rest, which he knew I could not have, as I had a business to look after and a very sick husband, so I carried on. Then in 1943 I had an internal haemorrhage and they sent me to hospital but they did not find the cause, just said I must rest for a month which I did as best I could. In 1953 I was taken very ill and rushed off to hospital for an operation for colostomy which at first I refused to have done as I knew what it meant, however as they said I could not live more than six weeks, for my sons' sake I consented but unfortunately collapsed half-way through the operation and so they had to leave a deep-seated cancer untouched, but did the colostomy. They told my sons I could not live more than eighteen months at the most, but I am still here and it is nearly two and a half years since then. I have had two minor operations since then, three in eleven months and twenty-two weeks in bed but as my heart is very bad, I cannot take the anaesthetic and so it is done by injections in the neck.

Now the surgeon tells me he can do no more for me until I become an emergency case, then it will be a fifty-fifty chance. But that does not worry me at all as it may never happen.

Every day I have to use a Wilston to keep the tubes open and about every six months I go to hospital and they break down the adhesions which form, otherwise I could not keep going. It is a painful job but one soon forgets it. Well, that is the history which I feel could have been prevented if taken in the early stages.

Please do not think I am unhappy or sorry for myself. I am very cheerful and enjoy my life as best I can. I have turned 72 and been a widow for nearly eight years and live by myself. I have a splendid doctor who comes to see me every fortnight, and my minister is so very kind, he comes seven miles to see me every week when I have to be in hospital. I belong to the Free Church and have been attending the same church for 46 years, quite a long time.

I hope that you will forgive me not answering your letter before, but I have been rather worried. My sister who is 74 is in hospital in London just had her 19th operation for the same trouble and I am going in a few days to look after her when she leaves hospital.

If only they could find the cause of this complaint, many lives would be saved I am sure. I personally think it is hereditary and appears in the third generation but the doctors differ very much about this. I trust I have not bored you too much with all this and I am quite sure that it won't be any use in your case book, only just another picture of what one can face up to and still be thankful to be alive and I am quite sure my own suffering has not been in vain but that is something I cannot divulge even to you. I pray you will continue to keep well and enjoy life and have many years before you to help cheer people up.

Sincerely yours,

Of course cancer is not catching so it was cruel of people to shun her and her idea that it is hereditary through the third generation is quite wrong.

Sometimes you hear of a person who has been declared a hopeless case, and the following illustration of someone now living very close to me in Bournemouth is of value. This lady at the age of forty-five had a really massive cancer of the chest which was growing rapidly. So big was it that it was impossible to operate and so she had the maximum dose of deep X rays. They came to the conclusion that they could not possibly do any more for her. She was sent down to Bournemouth as a hopeless case at the age of forty-seven. Here a wise doctor, who is a friend of mine, gave her a straightforward series of hormone doses. He visited her continuously and encouraged her to have faith and believe that she was going to get well.

Now, eight years later, she is living a practically normal life and you would never know to meet her that she had been through all this. No one really knows whether it was the hormones or self-limitation or antibodies which rose up within her to beat the cancer.

Here is another case of self-limiting cancer. An old lady from the Midlands, aged eighty-two, was sent down to Bournemouth five years ago with extensive cancer of the breast. She was so ill and frail that no operation was possible. Her weight dropped from eight stone to four and a half stone, which is considered to be incredible. After three years of treatment in the Midlands, she was sent to Bournemouth and, by some extraordinary series of circumstances which doctors cannot discover, gradually became well. The tumor has decreased in size. She lives a normal life and now weighs seven stone and is aged eighty-seven.

The problem of living, for us who suffer, or have cancer, is a curiously divided process, for outwardly we exhibit a happy and composed countenance—small surface amenities—whereas within there can be a raging torment of mind, body, and imagination. Like a yacht on the water, most of our keel and hull are below the surface, unseen by the outside world but battling out the process of living—keeping the boat upright and the gay coloured sails set.

The keel is a heavy weight indeed, and sometimes we wonder if we can drag ourselves along another step further, but along comes a puff of wind to test our faith and determination. We pull in the jib sheet, the limp lifeless sails tighten, and the incredible happens, for we have risen to the occasion and away we go. The keel is no longer a drag—it helps to speed us on our way by forcing the sails upright into the challenging wind.

To take to drink when the weight below seems too heavy to be borne would be all too easy, but it would court disaster. To take to drugs, except to dull the topmost moments of pain, would be to build up a hangover of depression and despair which would increase the weight below. The mast, with its stays to support it, points up to heaven and to God, and I must tend the stays, shackles, and shrouds to keep it ever thus. My "stays" are prayer, my Bible, and the holy mysteries of God which Christ himself gave us in the Communion bread and wine.

My mast must reach up and away from this heavy hull of my body to another world to enable me to meet the challenge of the wind and the weight of my boat beneath the surface. Through the mysterious unseen Holy Spirit of God I can feed my soul on His very body and blood—I can be identified in Christ and in His suffering. Then with the wings of a dove—with the sails of the most handsome yacht—I can fly away and send this creaking hull skimming through the deep waters. Although at times I feel afraid of all the things that I attempt and the boat seems sluggish in the water, I "up tiller" and know that tingling sensation of making headway against the elements.

I want so badly to go to Australia and to America again to preach and lecture. I plot and plan it in my mind. I take it as an accomplished fact that I am going as soon as I can

afford it. I have open preaching invitations in Florida,
New York, Colorado Springs, and California. Yet I sometimes feel afraid of such an undertaking, although I plan
to have my wife with me as my inseparable companion to
help me. Afraid of the difficulties of accommodation because of bad sleeping and the colostomy, and there rises
up a groundless mist of doubts and fears. But what are
these things in the mist? "Come, let me clutch thee. I have
thee not, and yet I see thee still." When I get up close to
them in the mist, I know that they are the same stupid
fears which try to prevent my accepting speaking and
other engagements right here and now. "Will I be well
enough?" "Will the insides behave or let me down?" "Get
thee behind me Satan—it has always been all right before."
So I pull in my invisible "jib sheets," "up tiller," and sail
right in, for life is too short and too exciting to let up and
paddle about in the shallows.

I am particularly pleased when casual acquaintances
think I look the picture of health as they find me mowing
endless lawns or swimming or rushing around London.

There are so many things in life for each one of us to
reach after, and I think it is right for the cancer patient as
for almost any sick person to hitch his wagon to the fur-
thest star and go out after it. Self-pity, overprudence, and
too much self-preservation can confine us to the prison of
inactivity. You know that wonderful proverb in the Bible:
"He that observeth the wind shall not sow; and he that
regardeth the clouds shall not reap."

The spirit of adventure and activity is vital to the patient and for the doctor.

How can you and I stoop down and rebuild our lives
with wornout bodies? May I remind you of what Paul said
when he was writing to the Church at Corinth and was
discussing the problem of his own infirmities and his "thorn
in the flesh," which tradition has come to believe to have

been blindness. He says in the eighth verse of the twelfth chapter of the Second Epistle to the Corinthians that he had besought the Lord three times to remove his thorn in the flesh. I suppose many people who have suffered have likewise asked God to take their suffering away, but for some strange, inexplicable reason the suffering goes on. They have to face up to the problem of living with it and conquering it.

So Paul goes on in the ninth verse and says how God whispered in his ear: "My grace is sufficient for thee: for my strength is made perfect in weakness." So, rising up from the embers of his life, Paul dragged his body across Europe and was an earthen vessel for God to use in his service. He had to prove that "all things work together for good to them that love God, to them who are the called according to his purpose."

If you turn back to the original Greek you will find that the meaning of this verse really is that in all things Christ is working for the good of the person who fulfils the conditions of this promise. You could almost go a stage further and say, "Despite the appearance of all things, I believe that Christ will bring good out of it if I love Him and if I am convinced that I am called by Him."

With this conviction we learn to say with Paul, "I can . . . through Christ which strengtheneth me."

This basic reliance on the unseen power of God, as Christ revealed Him, becomes the main springboard for the courage to reach out to the stars, whatever the physical disabilities. The courage to begin life in a different form all over again without whimpering is born of God deep down inside one. Every adversity is a challenge to step boldly out into the adventure of tomorrow with a conviction that we can do anything with the help of Christ.

I hope that many of you who read this book will find fresh courage and strengthened faith from its pages. Will you become a partner of this book and of its message for the human breast no matter whether cancer has brushed the arm of your family or not?

Not in any spirit of "I am better than thou," will you give it to your friends and see to it that it gets into every nook and cranny? Out of this, Cancer Anonymous will grow and spread throughout the world and unseen hands will be helping to alleviate this toll of human suffering. A snowball for God and man. Though you and I may never meet we have a fellowship together and we owe it to each other and to God to keep the flag of victory flying whatever our problem may be. . . .

BE DETERMINED TO LIVE